THE PRACTICE OF PUBLIC PR

CW01465492

THE PRACTICE OF
PUBLIC PROCUREMENT

Tendering, Selection and Award

Philipp KIIVER
Jakub KODYM

intersentia

Cambridge – Antwerp – Portland

Intersentia Ltd
Sheraton House | Castle Park
Cambridge | CB3 0AX | United Kingdom
Tel.: +44 1223 370 170 | Email: mail@intersentia.co.uk

Distribution for the UK:
NBN International
Airport Business Centre, 10 Thornbury Road
Plymouth, PL6 7 PP
United Kingdom
Tel.: +44 1752 202 301 | Fax: +44 1752 202 331
Email: orders@nbninternational.com

Distribution for the USA and Canada:
International Specialized Book Services
920 NE 58th Ave. Suite 300
Portland, OR 97213
USA
Tel.: +1 800 944 6190 (toll free)
Email: info@isbs.com

Distribution for Austria:
Neuer Wissenschaftlicher Verlag
Argentinierstraße 42/6
1040 Wien
Austria
Tel.: +43 1 535 61 03 24
Email: office@nwv.at

Distribution for other countries:
Intersentia Publishing nv
Groenstraat 31
2640 Mortsel
Belgium
Tel.: +32 3 680 15 50
Email: mail@intersentia.be

Dr Philipp Kiiver, LLM, and Jakub Kodym, MA, MBA, are procurement officers at the European Parliament in Luxembourg. This book is written in a strictly personal capacity, and does not purport to reflect the official opinion of the European Parliament or its administration.

Readers are encouraged to send the authors their comments, questions and suggestions by e-mail to feedback@pproc.eu.

The Practice of Public Procurement. Tendering, Selection and Award
Philipp Kiiver and Jakub Kodym

© 2014 Intersentia
Cambridge – Antwerp – Portland
www.intersentia.com | www.intersentia.co.uk

Cover image: Marsden Hartley (1877–1943), Abstraction – Wikimedia Commons

ISBN 978-1-78068-266-2
D/2014/7849/153
NUR 823

British Library Cataloguing in Publication Data. A catalogue record for this book is available from the British Library.

CONTENTS

TABLE OF CASES

EUROPEAN COURT OF JUSTICE
(ECJ OF THE COURT OF JUSTICE OF THE EU)

COURT OF FIRST INSTANCE / GENERAL COURT OF THE COURT OF JUSTICE OF THE EU

TABLE OF FIGURES

CHAPTER 1

INTRODUCTION

Public procurement is the acquisition by public authorities of goods and services through a public contract: for example the supply of office furniture for a government building, under a contract with a furniture store. To conclude such a contract, depending on the value and the applicable procurement law, the contracting authority normally publishes a call for tenders. This is an invitation for firms to submit tenders, or offers, and state under which conditions and for which prices they could supply what is needed. The publicity of calls for tenders is a way to ensure open and fair competition for public contracts, and efficient spending of public money. Having evaluated the tenders received, the contracting authority then chooses the best offer, and awards the contract to the winner who then becomes, in our example, the supplier of office furniture. But how exactly does the contracting authority decide what the best offer is? The consideration and evaluation of tenders is carried out in accordance with public procurement law, which sets the ground rules, but also in accordance with the conditions of the call for tenders itself. Thus, the contracting authority may have stated, in the call for tenders, that tendering firms must have a minimum annual turnover of ten million euros to be admissible, and that a preference will be given to furniture that has an eco-label. These are selection criteria and award criteria, respectively, which are drafted in advance by the contracting authority itself, and which are then used to admit or reject tenders. Yet such criteria must not only be lawful, they must also be appropriate. After all, inadequate criteria, even if they are not illegal as such, can still create unfair tendering conditions and lead to inefficient government spending. For example, is it really necessary in this case to insist on a minimum turnover, and thus to automatically reject smaller and medium-sized enterprises? If the eco-label is truly important to the contracting authority, perhaps it would make more sense to make it a mandatory technical requirement for *all* tenders, rather than an optional extra? Or perhaps the opposite is true: the contracting authority may not actually be willing to pay a higher price for its furniture just because it has an eco-label. But if the label has already been made an award criterion, it will necessarily justify a higher price: firms collecting points for this quality feature can afford to be more expensive on the price side. Yet if the contracting authority is in fact only interested in keeping the price low, it should simply award the contract to the lowest bidder. Whenever we draft tender documents – whether we are procurement officers, technicians, validators or any other actor involved in the design of a procurement process – we should keep in mind fairness and efficiency. This means, in this case, not disadvantaging firms for no good reason, and it means making sure that we do not end up paying too much on things we do not need.[1]

1.1. THE TENDERING PROCEDURE

Before we even reach the stage at which we apply substantive criteria to incoming tenders, we need to determine the procedural setup for our call for tenders. This is the framework in which we communicate with firms to begin with. In the above case of office furniture, for example, we would specify where interested companies can obtain the detailed tender documents, by what date they can ask questions, by what date they must submit their tender and in what form. Some procedural requirements are prescribed by public procurement law so as to ensure that tendering conditions are fair: for example, a typical rule is that there is a submission deadline, and that all tenders are opened simultaneously.

Yet there are also rules that contracting authorities are free to fix on their own, and here the main objective should be to keep things simple and inviting. Tendering documents could, for example, be sent to interested firms by registered mail, upon written request, for a fee; but they could also be put online for free, which is a much friendlier and a much more economical way of approaching the target audience. Deadlines sometimes have to be tight, but they should not be needlessly tight, because every firm that misses the deadline is a firm whose offer we will never see. Sometimes contracting authorities organize a visit to the premises, forcing potential tenderers to attend it before making an offer. This, too, can be justified in many cases, but should be avoided where possible because, among other things, it makes the tendering process more burdensome. Formalities must be respected where they are necessary, but the overall objective is to attract, not deter, potential tenderers.

---

[1] We speak of "buyers" or "procurement officers" in a broad sense. In fact we address any official who is involved in the design of procurement procedures, including purchasing and authorizing officers, lawyers, analysts, negotiators, consultants, etc. The terms "firms" and "companies" are used interchangeably to refer to economic operators; "tender" and "offer" are used synonymously as well. A "tenderer" is a firm that has submitted an offer, an "awardee" is a successful tenderer that has been awarded the contract, a "contractor" is an awardee whose contract has been signed. For technical terms we generally use EU procurement law terminology, but the same logic applies to all equivalent categories under national law, even if they are known under different names.

1.2. SELECTION CRITERIA

Under selection criteria, tendering firms have to show that they are, judging by their current situation, in principle capable of executing a contract: for example because they are large enough, financially healthy enough, experienced enough, or well enough equipped. Annual turnover, as used in the above example about the office furniture contract, is in fact a typical selection criterion regarding financial capacity. Selection criteria are thus applied to the tendering firms themselves, not to the content of their offers. They can take the form of a yes/no selection for sufficient or insufficient capacity, or a ranking of the most and the least capable firms to be invited to a next stage in the award procedure.

In both cases, the main danger of ill-designed selection criteria is that we impose standards that are too strict, or too lenient, or that either way have little to do with the actual object of the contract. This in turn can mean that we needlessly reject tenderers who would have had sufficient capacity, or that we accept firms that do not, or both. In our example above, turnover as an indicator of a company's size could be a useful criterion for a long-term, high-volume contract, where contractors will need to be able to handle large clients, purchase large volumes of merchandise themselves before getting paid, and to absorb these costs. In the case of a single one-off supply of a single item of furniture, however, turnover is not necessarily useful as a selection criterion, and may even become unfair: if there is no proper justification resulting from a risk assessment, the criterion will just needlessly exclude smaller companies from the tendering process. Sometimes selection criteria are used to make sure that firms are financially healthy, and will not go bankrupt three months into the contract; for that, however, turnover is not a good indicator at all, because it indicates size not health. To assess the financial health of companies, a different approach is needed. We recommend choosing selection criteria that are tailored to identified risks of contract performance, and we will provide examples which criteria are useful and which ones are not.

1.3. TECHNICAL SPECIFICATIONS

Technical specifications describe the content of the performance that firms must offer, and that they then must execute in case they are awarded the contract. The question here is therefore not whether the firm is capable to execute the contract, but whether it is actually offering what we are looking for. Here the main danger is that the specifications are drafted too narrowly, so that competition is limited because only a single provider or a single brand can possibly comply with the technical requirements. In our office furniture example above, if we simply copy the dimensions of a table that we saw in a catalogue, and turn them into technical requirements, we easily end up excluding all competition. Thus, a cheaper desk, but of the same quality as our preferred brand, may get rejected just because it is 5 cm too long. Unless the dimensions need to be precise for objective reasons, narrowing down specifications to those of a favoured brand is unfair, costly, harmful and potentially illegal. We advocate an ends-based approach to the drafting of technical specifications, which means to define our needs, and to leave it to firms to propose possible solutions. In addition, we will discuss how to effectively use options, variants, and the possibility for one firm to submit several tenders, in order to encourage healthy competition even more.

1.4. AWARD CRITERIA

Award criteria are used to determine which tender is successful and who receives the contract. When drafting such award criteria, contracting authorities must make the most complex choices. We must first of all decide whether we want to award the contract to the lowest bidder, based on the offer's price or cost. In that case, we have only a single award criterion, and the cheapest offer wins. Alternatively, we can evaluate not only the price but also the quality that is offered for that price, and thus award the contract to the tenderer offering the best price-quality ratio. This means that the contract can go to a bidder who is more expensive, but who offers a higher quality to justify the price. If we opt for a price-quality award, we must determine on which quality criteria we want tenderers to compete, and what weight the price and the quality should have in the evaluation. The price weight indicates to firms how important it is to us that they be cheap; the weight of the quality criterion is determined by the extra cost that we are willing to accept in order to obtain better quality instead of basic quality. Thus, in our office furniture example, we need to decide whether we want to describe exhaustively what quality we need and then purchase the cheapest furniture as long as it meets these technical requirements, or whether we are willing to pay a basic price for basic materials and more for high-quality materials, and, if so, how much more. The danger of ill-chosen award methods is that we pay too much because our award criteria, and the formulas that we use to relate quality scores to the price, do not accurately reflect our needs and preferences. In this book we will propose concrete formulas, illustrated with practical examples, how to calculate the value of an authority's wishes and to weight them appropriately. Based on a fair and objective price-quality ratio, in effect simply quality divided by price but adjusted for the weighting, our recommendations should help contracting authorities get the best quality for the money they spend, without overspending on things that they do not actually need.

1.5. EUROPEAN UNION LAW

Although in this book we make frequent reference to EU case-law and procurement legislation, notably the 2014 Public Procurement Directive,[2] our recommendations and guidelines are largely independent of the legislative framework and apply within basically any system. As to the European Union, the general rule is that EU member states have to use the award procedures specified in the EU Directive for awards above certain value thresholds, and that they can each fix their own national rules for awards below these thresholds.[3] Still, whether national or European, the basic logic of public buying will mostly be the same. For example, under EU law it is illegal to evaluate firms' technical capacity at the award stage, because this is something that must be checked at an earlier stage, using selection criteria.[4] However, even if it *were* legal to double-check firms' capacity like that, it is simply not a good idea. After all, it means giving quality points to companies for something that is already confirmed, for no reason. As a result, all tenders will receive similar quality scores. And with quality differences almost cancelled out, the price will decide, which is not what we wanted in this case because otherwise we would have chosen a lowest-bid award. Thus we risk ending up buying the cheapest product with the poorest quality, simply because we evaluated the same thing twice.

1.6. SOUND FINANCIAL MANAGEMENT

Criteria and tendering process design in general must not only be lawful, it must also comply with principles of sound financial management. In other words, procurement design must help us seize economic opportunities and limit inefficiency. Design choices should therefore translate true preferences into clear and predictable tendering conditions. Whether we buy office furniture, lease a car park, or order the construction of a tunnel through a mountain, we should in

---

2   Directive 2014/24/EU of 26 February 2014 on public procurement and repealing Directive 2004/18/EC, OJ L 94/65.
3   See also Chr. Bovis, *EU Public Procurement Law*, 2nd ed., Cheltenham: Edward Elgar 2012; S. Arrowsmith, 'EC Regime on Public Procurement', in K. Thai, ed., *International Handbook of Public Procurement*, Boca Raton: CRC Press 2009; P. Trepte, *Public Procurement in the EU – A Practitioner's Guide*, 2nd ed., Oxford: OUP 2007. EU institutions themselves, in their capacity as contracting authorities, are governed by a set of EU Regulations which however largely follow the logic of the Directive that applies to member states.
4   Case C-31/87 *Beentjes*. All cited case-law refers to rulings of the Court of Justice (case numbers starting with the letter C), and the Court of First Instance or General Court of the Court of Justice of the European Union (case numbers starting with the letter T). Even with the clarification in Article 67 (2) (b) of Directive 2014/24/EU that CVs of team members can be reviewed at the award stage if this has a quality impact, analysis at the award stage must be strictly separate from capacity analysis at the selection stage.

each case determine what we need, what kind of firms we want to deal with, what the best offer is according to our priorities, and be clear and open about it.

Actually, what *are* our needs and priorities? This should be evaluated and formulated for each new contract. Simply copying the terms of the previous call for tenders with the same object creates the risk of perpetuating an unsatisfactory situation or the use of outdated solutions. Indeed, there are cases of recurring contracts – for example the same maintenance or supply contract that gets re-awarded every few years, or standard consultancy work or research studies – where the procurement routine has not changed in decades. The same definitions, the same selection criteria, even the same award criteria with the same weighting. However, each new award is a new opportunity to improve the goods and services we obtain. If there is a pre-existing contract, we must ask: What has proven to work well? What were the main weaknesses last time? Where did our colleagues constantly have to double-check? Has there been any dispute over unclear contract provisions? And we must direct all these questions not only to the operational managers, but also to the people in the field: engineers, drivers, users of office furniture. In addition, it may be that our historical contracts no longer match our organization's strategy, for example because there is now a stronger focus on synergies with other organizations, on a reduction of waste, on public transport which requires fewer contracts for the building of parking lots, or on leaner stocks of supplies which in turn require more flexible delivery solutions. A new call for tenders is a good moment to check what innovations have appeared on the market in the meantime.

Once we do know what we want, we need to explain this to firms. Some procurement regimes and practices come across as highly bureaucratic and uninviting from companies' point of view.[5] That is because there are public authorities which treat procurement primarily as an administrative process, and which treat firms like applicants who come asking for a permit. Let us not forget, though, that often we need *them* more than they need us; at least we have an interest in making a successful award, because otherwise we find ourselves without a contractor. Furthermore, while contracting authorities may be bureaucracies, we should remember that we are still basically purchasing goods and services on the market. We, too, are economic operators. As a result, the guiding principles of public buying should come as close as possible to what is common sense in normal private buying. Invitations should be inviting: friendly, frank and straightforward. Preliminary market research should probe what is available in general, while negotiations, where they are permitted, should explore how offers could match demand even better. The point is to agree, to sign, to buy, not to find a reason to reject a company. Formal procurement rules are sometimes imposed by law, but sometimes *we* impose them, and when we do impose them, we should know exactly what they are for.

---

5   K. Lundvall, J. Tops & H. Ballebye Olesen, *What can public procurers learn from private?*, Copenhagen Economics 2008, p. 26.

CHAPTER 2

THE TENDERING PROCEDURE

The procedural setup forms part of the overall design of a procurement process, in that it determines the way the contracting authority communicates with companies. The setup includes, for example, the way companies can obtain the tender documents and ask questions, or the submission deadline for tenders.

Some conditions are imposed by law, others are managed by contracting authorities themselves. As a general rule, when designing a procedural setup, we should remember to keep requirements simple, the rules transparent, and entry costs for participating companies low.[1] The higher we make the administrative burden on tendering firms, the more we favour the biggest firms, or firms that are close to us because they already work for us, and the more we exclude everyone else. Economists speak of transaction costs, or the cost of making a market transaction, meaning in this case the cost for a firm to go through our procurement process to begin with. Turning a call for tenders into a bureaucratic nightmare raises transaction costs, and thus it discourages companies that could have made a good offer, so we will never actually see their offer. Even the EU Public Procurement Directive itself explicitly identifies administrative burden, in other words red tape, to be a major obstacle to participation in tendering procedures, not least for small and medium-sized enterprises.[2] If bureaucracy discourages companies from tendering, then in the end, among other things, we pay a higher price to someone else under conditions of weak competition, or we have to cancel the call because we did not receive any offers at all. Keeping it simple and straightforward is a fine way of lowering transaction costs, and of making life easier for both the seller and the buyer.

Some formalities are necessary to ensure fair competition and to prevent the misuse of public money, of course. For example, tenders may not be evaluated if they have not respected the submission deadline;[3] and, if the procedure is a sealed-bid award without negotiation, tenderers may not add things to their offer

---

[1]   S. Onderstal & F. Felsö, 'Procurement Design: Lessons from Economic Theory and Illustrations from the Dutch Procurement of Welfare-to-Work Projects', in K. Thai, ed., *International Handbook of Public Procurement*, Boca Raton: CRC Press 2009.

[2]   Recital 84 of the Preamble to Directive 2014/24/EU.

[3]   See case T-70/05 *Evropaiki Dynamiki/EMSA*, par. 104.

after the opening.[4] But then these formalities do have a real purpose: formalities should not exist just for their own sake.

2.1. ADVERTISEMENT

One of the most fundamental requirements to ensure a healthy competition is that calls for tenders be adequately advertised. Firms must know that somewhere a contracting authority intends to award a contract, so that they can decide whether to submit a tender or not. In the case of the European Union, the most basic form of publicity for high-value contracts is the standard contract notice, which is published in the Official Journal and which is accessible online free of charge. It summarizes the object and scope of the award, and states the basic tendering conditions such as the submission deadline. Equivalent obligations to publish notices exist under national procurement law. Sometimes the mandatory publicity may be perceived as a formality, but we should not forget that it is in *our* interest to have a wide publicity for our calls. It increases our chances to receive more offers than we would otherwise get, allowing us to obtain better quality, better prices, or both. Putting an EU contract notice online takes five minutes, but it draws the attention of more potentially interested companies to our call.

What other means are there to ensure sufficient publicity? Contract notices on official procurement platforms can reach certain companies, notably big ones which pay for media monitoring. But many small and medium-sized enterprises may not necessarily read them. The risk is then that the only companies that will have heard of the call for tenders are our "usual suspects", meaning companies which we already know because they already work for us. They are not necessarily the best, though, or they may have become worse over time. In order to reach more and newer competitors, we should consider other, supplementary forms of publicity. These may include advertisements in local or regional media, notices in trade fair catalogues and specialized professional magazines, or bulletins which professional boards or chambers of commerce can distribute among their members. In some cases it would be disproportionate to pay to place any ads, and a normal official notice is sufficient. In many other cases the advertisement is surely worth the fee. An intermediate solution is to place a single yearly advertisement of our forthcoming contracts, so that interested firms can keep track of specific calls for tenders during the year. Contracting authorities of a certain size may also create social-media and instant message posting accounts, attracting companies as subscribers which will then follow its posts about upcoming calls for tenders.

---

[4]   See cases C-87/94 *Commission v. Belgium*, T-461/08 *Evropaiki Dynamiki v. EIB*, par. 182.

What should a newspaper advertisement or an official contract notice look like? In some countries it is usual to name the object of the contract and barely anything else apart from the authority's contact address; in others contract notices in newspapers as well as in official bulletins tend to be extremely detailed, quoting full admissibility criteria and administrative provisions. We propose focusing on the core purpose of an ad, which is to draw firms' attention to a call and invite them to access the tender documents. In order to decide whether it is even worth the effort to access the documents, firms should have – and ads should give – a general idea of the contract: subject-matter, size (in terms of volume, working days or value), place of performance and basic time schedule, and qualification requirements, meaning a summary of selection criteria. Thus, it should not be too short, but not as extensive as is sometimes the case either.

The cost of publicity should be weighed against the extra market efficiency that we generate through more competition. The administrative cost of having to treat an excessive number of incoming tenders is certainly part of the cost as well, but this is not handled by keeping publicity low: it is handled by clear tendering conditions, such as appropriate and comprehensible selection criteria, making sure that only firms with the right capacity will tender. In any event, the purpose should never be publicity simply for the sake of complying with procurement law. The purpose is to attract interest, invite companies, and thereby stimulate competition.

How about contacting firms directly? There are procedures where the contracting authority approaches and invites potential tenderers directly, so broader publicity becomes complementary. But in the two standard types of procurement procedures for high-value contracts under the EU Public Procurement Directive, namely the open and the restricted procedure, for example, such direct approaching of firms is not specifically regulated. On the one hand, contacting favoured firms might give them an information advantage over everyone else, thereby potentially distorting competition. On the other hand, though, a broad, justified, non-discriminatory and well-documented direct advertisement campaign can actually *stimulate* competition, where otherwise some firms may not have tendered at all. If market research shows that there are four market leaders in the installation of certain equipment, plus an unknown number of other companies in the same line of business, why not send at least these known market participants an e-mail? This seems particularly important if in fact there are *only* four firms on the market: if even one of them misses the call, we will already have lost 25% of competition. Direct contact at the launch of a call should of course not give firms any information that is not also publicly available, and it cannot replace wider publicity where such wider publicity is prescribed. All it would say is: good morning, we draw your attention to our call for tenders, and we invite you to consult the tender documents. This not only allows firms to take note of a call they may otherwise have missed, it also encourages them to actually tender. That is because the signal that we send is in fact very positive: it means we have not just published a contract notice because we had to, as a pure formality, but we actually do want competition and we are curious about their offer. This is not some dubious deal where we already know the winner: this is an actual, open, competitive procurement procedure, and it is open for business.

2.2. PUBLICATION OF TENDER DOCUMENTS

Notices, such as the contract notices published in the Official Journal of the European Union for EU-wide procurement, other notices on national or regional online procurement platforms, or newspaper ads, are all means to draw firms' attention to a call for tenders. They are however only short summaries of the call. In order to prepare an actual tender, a firm needs to obtain the full tender documents including the detailed technical specifications.

It is a very welcome development that more and more contracting authorities use e-tendering tools, whereby firms can access the full tender documents online, and download them free of charge. Typically a firm simply needs to register, for free, on an internet site, and then receives alerts and obtains access to tender documents for calls that are potentially interesting to it. Some contracting authorities even put their tender documents online completely openly, for example on the respective municipality's normal website, so that firms do not even have to register to download them. All these are highly efficient ways to inform companies about a call for tenders, and the conditions for tendering, while keeping entry costs practically at zero. If the main form of advertisement is a contract notice or a newspaper ad, it would refer to the URL where the full documents can be obtained. A short URL that can be easily typed over from print media is ideal; if the URL is too long, URL shorteners are available, although free solutions may not always guarantee permanence and sufficient data protection, so an internal shortener or a paid service would in that case be advisable. The full URL should be printed in any case, to be sure.

There are however still cases where the notice simply directs firms which wish to obtain the full tender documents to the office in charge of the call for tenders, for example the municipal procurement unit. Firms can then request the full documents with that office, sometimes after paying an administrative fee. This is highly regrettable, because in most cases such barriers to market participation, especially fees, should be avoidable. In general, a small administrative fee can cover the cost of printing and posting tender documents, while discouraging frivolous requests. Printing and posting costs are very relevant when tender documents are voluminous, and include detailed construction plans printed on oversize paper sheets or saved on physical CDs.

But irrespective of the volume, printing and posting costs can be neutralized by simply putting the documents online. In that case reading them costs nothing, while the costs of actually printing them are borne by the firms themselves, if they want to print them. This saves the contracting authority time and money, while again keeping entry costs low for all interested firms. If the available e-tendering platform has limitations on the size of files, accessory documents like oversize plans and pictures can be posted on either internal or external commercial file repositories. If, one way or the other, a firm experiences technical problems with the download, it should still be able to ask for the paper version – in which case it may have to pay a fee, because now there is an actual cost. If the contracting authority does not want to post the documents itself or to process the payment of fees, it can also direct firms to a professional printer, so that they can pick up their documents and pay for them right there. Firms that can download documents on their own will not need the paper version, and so can avoid the fee altogether. In cases where a website is not available, or an upload would not be justified considering the limited nature of the call, the full documents could still be sent to requesting firms via e-mail. This costs virtually nothing compared with a paper dispatch, and does not need to be covered by a fee either.

And even if the contracting authority cannot use e-mail, or if it insists on paper dispatch for some other reason, we wonder if it is really necessary to ask a fee. For a municipality, for example, the costs of sending out tender documents will unlikely be a significant proportion of all its ordinary outgoing paper mail. If the authority actually *does* spend much money on paper, envelopes and post stamps to send out tender documents, we suggest that this is all the more reason to activate an online portal for free downloads, or to join an existing one. The costs even of installing a new online portal are minimal, as long as the authority simply buys a ready-made, off-the-shelf solution that is cheap, tried and tested.

2.3. THE STYLE OF TENDER DOCUMENTS

A subtle but important difference between calls for tenders lies in the language in which they are written. By this we mean the style in which the tender documents are drawn up. Ideally, they are written in a clear, honest, and logical way so that they are easy to read. The opposite would be tender documents that come across as bureaucratic, because they are heavy on legal conditions and threats, listing almost with delight all the possible reasons for which tenders might be rejected. Let us be clear: tendering conditions must be transparent in advance, so that firms cannot be rejected for reasons they did not know existed. But there is a stylistic difference between inviting and threatening calls, even where their content is identical. For example, "We invite you to make an offer, the submission deadline is 26 September" is much more welcoming than "Tenderers must submit their offer by 26 September, failure to comply with the deadline results in the rejection of offers."

Furthermore, tenders often must include supporting documentation, such as a financial statement or an excerpt from the register of commerce. It is helpful to either summarize all documents that must be included in a checklist for tenderers, or to state immediately, under each relevant section, which proofs are required for what criterion. The reward for clearly structured and user-friendly tender documents is a higher chance of receiving clearly structured, user-friendly, and above all complete tenders in return.

2.4. PUBLISHING THE CONTRACT VALUE ESTIMATE

Should we publish the value of the contract in the call for tenders or not? That depends on what message we wish to send to tenderers, and what incentive we wish to set for them. What we evidently want to avoid is that firms, instead of making competitive price offers, take our estimate as a starting point and calculate their prices from there. In negotiations for the purpose of private buying, for instance, it is a golden rule *not* to disclose in the beginning how much you are willing to pay. Especially in markets with limited competition, companies might otherwise be able to afford to inflate their prices to match our published estimate.

At the same time it is in our own interest to communicate to potential tenderers the approximate scale of the contract, so that they will know what kind of volume will be purchased and in what range their turnover will likely be. At the very basic, they should understand immediately whether it is a "big", "medium" or "small" contract, which among other things helps them determine whether unit prices can be lowered to accommodate a large customer generating economies of scale. Wherever it is possible, we precisely recommend expressing the scope of the contract in terms of volume, and not in terms of money: we will be needing between 100 and 120 vehicles over three years; the works include the replacement of 15 heating units in five different buildings; the cleaning contract covers 20,000 square metres of office space.

There are cases where publishing an overall money amount is nevertheless the most straightforward means to help tenderers understand the scope of the contract. We could think of framework contracts with a highly complex price schedule consisting of hundreds or thousands of items, where it may be easier to simply say that this is a framework contract of, roughly, 5 million euros over four years. Another example could be research studies, where, instead of writing several pages of description, we could simply state that the target price is

€20,000, which again gives a much more immediate idea of the scope. In fact, we might even decide to not let tenderers compete on price at all. If prices are regulated or otherwise fixed anyway, there is by definition no price competition; yet in quality-heavy contracts it is equally possible to fix and publish the budget in advance, and allow competition to focus exclusively on quality.[5]

In cases where we want to give an indication of the contract's monetary value, without however being too precise about it, there remains the possibility to publish a price range. A food supplies contract might thus be worth between 1 and 2 million euros a year. If we do that, however, we should also be clear about what that range actually represents, meaning what exactly determines the borders. Why is it between 1 and 2 million? Are prices in the market for food generally spread between 1 and 2 million, even for otherwise equivalent products? Or are we simply uncertain about market prices? Or will we in principle be ordering food worth 1 million, but might potentially need twice as much food? Or are we willing to pay 1 million for basic food and up to 2 million for food that is of higher quality, in accordance with our award criteria?[6]

The clearer our needs are expressed, the fairer competition will be; the more opaque we are in our description and estimates, the more we risk either receiving offers that do not accurately match our needs, which will cause problems later on, or advantaging insider companies that already know us. In the case of scale estimates, we recommend volume estimates instead of money estimates, unless the price schedule is too complex for a reliable quantitative estimate, or unless we want to eliminate or strongly limit price competition in order to focus on quality competition.

2.5. QUESTIONS AND ANSWERS

Before they submit their tenders, firms typically have an opportunity to ask questions to clarify certain elements from the call for tenders. The process of questions and answers should follow the principle of equal treatment of tenderers, meaning notably that at least questions of a broader interest, and the corresponding answers, should be made available to all firms, not just those who asked the question. That is because the answer to a particular question can have an impact on the meaning of certain details in the call, or actually change their meaning, so all potential tenderers should be aware of this. Naturally any published question should be anonymized.

Sometimes questions draw our attention to mistakes we had made, so our answer is a good occasion to clarify. Some procurement officers might take a strict approach to questions and answers, setting a tight deadline for the receipt

---

5   See, for example, Article 67 (2) of Directive 2014/24/EU and Chapter 8.8 below.
6   See Chapter 8.3 below.

of questions for example, way ahead of the submission deadline. However, by asking questions firms are basically doing us a favour, because they allow us to check again for correctness what we had published. No matter how many times we check in advance, there can always be a mistake in the call, or something that is correct but formulated in an ambiguous manner. We should therefore be grateful for the questions we receive about this. Think, for example, of the following types of questions: "On page 5 it says 300 cm, but on page 12 it says 320 cm; which one is correct?"; "It says that the minimum is 7 mm, but is there also a maximum?"; "Are you sure you mean a 700 litre unit, it seems a bit much." Having this clarified saves firms headaches at drawing up a tender, and it saves us headaches when reviewing tenders in the end: "Sorry, the correct dimension is indeed 320 cm", and "Yes, there is a maximum, and it is 9 mm".

Sometimes a firm might use its questions to actually propose an alternative or additional solution, and inquire whether we are interested in that one, too. Yes, they are pitching us something else from their catalogue. But again, let us not forget that we may be in public procurement, but we are still basically sellers and buyers. And in a normal sale on the normal market it is perfectly fine, and even welcome, to hear that other products exist as well. We may not be able to accept any supplement if this would change too much the initial tendering conditions – this would be unfair to firms which did not respond to the first call but which may have responded to a call under different circumstances. But still we should be grateful for firms' attempts at communicating with us like they would with a normal client.

The considerations on the fairness of changing tendering conditions should essentially guide us when we adjust some technical detail in the call. We should not completely arbitrarily change the content of the call, of course, by ordering chairs instead of desks, for instance. But we should not be afraid of some fine-tuning either. For example: "Yes, the maximum is 9 mm" is a technical adjustment. So is "Yes, 700 litres is correct, but a smaller unit is also acceptable as a technically equivalent solution", and it may well be an appropriate precision. The only question is: would a different firm have shown interest had it known the new details? If yes, then a change via questions and answers is unfair, and the change should be announced more broadly, in the way the original call had been published: in the case of a contract notice, by means of a rectification or a new call. However, if the group of interested firms would remain the same one way or the other, there is nothing truly objectionable about some fine-tuning. Depending on the procedure, the group of interested firms comprises those firms that had requested the tender specifications, or those that had downloaded them from an e-tendering platform, or those that had been invited to tender, or those that had shown up for a mandatory visit to the premises. We must not unduly put firms at a disadvantage, but we should also keep our other interest in mind: the interest to buy something that fulfils our technical needs. Holding back information at the questions-and-answers stage will result in tenders that are not precisely suited to our needs. This will be frustrating for the firms, and it will be frustrating for us.

2.6. VISITS TO THE PREMISES

In works contracts, but also for instance in the case of supplies where machinery needs to be installed, a contracting authority may demand that tenderers inspect the location where the work is to take place before they submit their bid. This then becomes a mandatory visit to the premises. The underlying thought is to force firms to get a realistic picture of the scope and environment of the envisaged performance before making an offer. Firms that did not take part in a mandatory visit may not tender.

There is, however, an inherent risk in insisting on such visits. First, such an event adds time and travel expenses for a potential tenderer. This may deter firms, especially those at a greater geographical distance, from participating in the call, so competition is already limited. The winning tenderer, meanwhile, will add the expenses to the price. If we are buying something for €5,000, and a tenderer has already spent €600 on train tickets and daily allowances to visit the premises, the price will of course be closer to €5,600. It is the authority that pays in the end.

Second, at least if there is one visit for all, it allows firms to see each other. Thus they will know how many competitors there are in total, and perhaps that they are the only firm to have shown up; if there are others present, they will know their identity and perhaps notice that an important competitor is absent. In these cases there is a higher risk that firms coordinate their bids, or that they otherwise do not make their best offer.

Third, even if we either disregard or accept these consequences, the insistence on a mandatory visit to the premises turns any award into a two-stage procedure. The group of potential tenderers is in the end limited to those firms that had attended the visit. We will never see the tenders of those that had not attended. If a visit is justified, we might say that we would not have wanted to see those offers anyway, since the firms submitting them had not visited the premises, so they do not know what they are tendering for. However, if a visit could have been avoidable, the field of players is needlessly closed after the visit has taken place. Without the visit, the field would have remained open until the submission deadline. We will never know who else might have used this extra time to draw up a tender. Competition is in fact restricted further the farther away the visit is from the submission deadline: if the overall tendering period is, say, 30 days, a mandatory visit 20 days before the deadline can easily be disproportionate, if it is enough to foresee a total of merely ten days for post-visit questions-and-answers and tender finalization. Ten days before the deadline should in that case be soon enough: like any excessively short deadline, too early a visit may not only limit the overall number of tenders, but in particular favour insiders.

Thus, if the purpose of the visit can just as well be served by including pictures and plans of the premises in the tender documents, then this should be preferred over a visit. If a visit is necessary, we should consider alternatives to an obligatory visit, such as an optional visit only for those who are interested, or separate visits for different firms so that they do not meet there, with fixed dates or a timeframe for visits on appointment. We can never completely guarantee that firms will not talk to each other, but at least we can refrain from facilitating such encounters.

2.7. DEADLINES

Regarding deadlines, save for minimum periods for the reception of tenders laid down in legislation,[7] it is in principle up to contracting authorities to allow for sufficient time for enough firms to prepare candidacies or expressions of interest and to submit their bids. Short deadlines allow for quick awards, but they limit competition to those who are contacted first, those who are first to know, and those who are first to have their tender ready. These tend to be incumbent contractors and otherwise "usual suspects".[8] From a contracting authority's point of view, limited competition means, quite practically – apart from the legal implications – fewer offers, less choice, and a higher risk of having to pay more than is necessary. We should remember that even statutory minimum deadlines are really *minimum* deadlines. It is absolutely legitimate to allow for some more time than that, and to also take into account, for example, summer holidays or the Christmas period when firms may be understaffed or busy. In general, if there is no urgency, it is better to wait.

2.8. TRANSMISSION FORMALITIES

As regards the tenders themselves, formal requirements are typically imposed for the format of their transmission, at least in the case of contracts with a higher value. This very much depends on the legislative framework and the internal policy of a contracting authority. The most straightforward transmission method is presumably a simple letter, or an even simpler e-mail, from the tenderer to the

---

[7] In open procedures under Article 27 of Directive 2014/24/EU, for example, the minimum delay between the dispatch of the contract notice and the submission deadline is in principle 35 days.

[8] Deadlines may not be fixed so as to favour a specific tenderer, see case T-415/10 *Nexans*.

authority, with the offer attached. At the more cumbersome end of the scale are tenders submitted on hard copy in sealed double envelopes, in triplicate or more. E-submission through a secure and authenticated upload should largely replace paper transmission. But whatever the available methods, especially when we have some freedom to determine formalities ourselves, we should always ask ourselves what the purpose of such formalities is.

Tenderers have an interest that no-one can see their price before the simultaneous opening of all tenders, so the insistence on sealed double envelopes, or a secure upload for everyone, is mostly a favour to firms, not to us. In addition, both the firms and the contracting authority have an interest in preventing anyone from manipulating a tender after the opening, for example by swapping a page for another which states a different price. But this is an anti-fraud measure tackled by a transparent and reliable opening and archiving routine, not by requiring thicker envelopes. The insistence on the transmission of several copies of each tender may sometimes be useful, but it creates extra costs and a risk of discrepancies between copies, and we should consider whether a single original might not be enough. If we need copies, we could scan them ourselves, or request tenders on USB sticks, with only a few key pages signed on actual paper.[9] When a tender is requested from a monopolist, like an electricity supplier or an existing contractor with an exclusive right, then there is hardly any point at all in prescribing specific formats or even deadlines. Since there is only one candidate, notions like confidentiality of transmission and simultaneous opening have no or very little meaning. If the monopolist answers too late, what are we going to do – reject him? Any transmission requirements should be related and proportionate to legitimate concerns. High-stakes contracts for multi-million euro construction works call for a different degree of formalization than a local low-value supply deal. Since formalities are essentially responses to risks, the lower the risk we are facing, the more leniency we can apply when it comes to formalities.

2.9. EXCLUSION CRITERIA

Another test, required or permitted at least under EU procurement law, is the application of exclusion criteria.[10] These are meant to prevent certain categories of firms from participating in award procedures to begin with, such as those that are being wound up or those that are subject to a criminal or administrative sanction. Since these are criteria that are not typically chosen or designed by

---

9   A practitioner told us that a high-tech firm had once proposed transmitting its tender saved on an iPad, which would have been easiest for them. Not entirely unproblematic if we get to keep the storage device, we agree, but charming.

10   Article 57 of Directive 2014/24/EU.

contracting authorities, but rather imposed by law, we will not discuss them in detail. We merely note that, where contracting authorities have a choice regarding the *proofs* that firms do not fall under exclusion cases, they should act in such way as to keep competition open and to address relevant risks. It is not always warranted to demand full proofs from all tenderers: a check only on the presumed winner may be enough. Conversely, where several phases of selection or negotiation take place, firms that should actually have been excluded at the start should not be allowed to stay in the game and influence other tenderers' bids, or displace others where the number of selected participants has been limited.

2.10. THE LENGTH OF VALIDITY OF TENDERS

Tenderers typically have to specify for how long their offer is valid, or commit to a binding period during which they must accept the award under the conditions of the initial tender. Here it is important to remember what the purpose of the validity period actually is. During the period itself, it protects the buyer, because award winners cannot claim that prices have risen in the meantime. After its expiry, it protects the tenderers: when their offer has expired, a firm cannot be forced to accept a contract based, for example, on last year's prices.

Yet while the tender validity period protects the buyer, and while in public procurement the buyer typically determines this period, fixing an excessively long validity period is not necessarily a good idea. In markets where prices do tend to rise, a company which sees that any offer must be valid for a whole year may decide not to tender at all. Otherwise it risks in the end indeed supplying a product at prices from a year ago, or carrying out services at prices that had been calculated on the basis of last year's labour costs. Those companies that *do* tender will presumably factor in the long validity period, and offer a higher price in order to compensate for the expected rises in costs. Tender validity periods should not just be as long as possible, but truly reflect the expected maximum duration of a procurement process. Otherwise competition is weakened and contracts become needlessly expensive.

What if, due to unforeseen delays, we do not actually manage to make the award within the validity period of the tenders received? It would seem strange for us to expect that all tenderers must unanimously agree to extend the validity of their respective offers. Since, as noted, the expiry of the period protects the seller, it should be up to each tenderer individually to extend the validity of his or her original offer or not. If a firm feels that its initial prices are still sustainable, it may agree to an extension; if it concludes that it is not worth it, it may withdraw the offer by refusing to prolong it. Only those tenderers that accept the prolongation will thus remain in the process.

Since the request to prolong can potentially be abused to distort competition – think of a process where firms are repeatedly asked to prolong until only the favoured firm is left – this option should be used with great diligence, under internal anti-corruption safeguards, and only in exceptional cases. When negotiations are available in the procurement procedure, the contracting authority might instead consider turning the request to prolong the validity of tenders into a negotiation round: asking all tenderers to update their offer, adjusting their quality upwards to increase value, or downwards to save money, and to re-calculate their price offers according to the updated pricing policy. This allows the contracting authority not only to buy time, but also to obtain an even better match between supply and demand, without losing any tenderers due to expired tender validity.

CHAPTER 3

TECHNICAL SPECIFICATIONS

Strictly speaking, firms first have to pass selection criteria, and only then are their tenders compared with the technical specifications, even though the 2014 EU Public Procurement Directive allows, in open procedures, to verify capacity under selection criteria for the presumed winner at the end.[1] Still, one way or the other, in practice a procurement officer will typically first draft the technical specifications, and only then design selection criteria depending on what is in the specs. This is why we will discuss technical specifications first. Tenders are reviewed against them in order to check their technical compliance, i.e. to make sure that the tenderer is offering what the contracting authority is asking for. If a firm passes the selection criteria but offers fluorescent lights instead of LED lights, or chairs instead of tables, or LED lights of the wrong voltage, or tables of the wrong material, then its tender is eliminated due to technical non-compliance. This is a test not of technical quality, but of sheer admissibility.

3.1. TECHNICAL REQUIREMENTS

How to draft technical specifications? Assume that a municipality wishes to install a set of security gates at the exit of a public library. The gates should set off an alarm whenever someone tries to steal a book. The procurement officer takes the catalogue of a big manufacturer of security gates, and types over the technical specifications of the model that he or she likes: height, detection range, electromagnetic frequency. Since at least under EU procurement law it is normally illegal to specify a brand,[2] in order not to restrict competition, the officer leaves out the brand name and launches a call for tenders.

While this is clearly the easiest way to draft technical specifications, it results in specifications that are most likely to limit competition to a single or a few providers. This not only means the automatic exclusion of possible competitors in breach of procurement law.[3] From the contracting authority's point of view, it also means an increased likelihood of paying too much for what could be

---

[1]   Article 57 (2) of Directive 2014/24/EU.
[2]   Article 42 (4) of Directive 2014/24/EU.
[3]   See also cases C-359/93 *Commission v. Netherlands* and C-59/00 *Vestergaard*.

obtained more cheaply, not to mention the missed opportunity to let other firms present innovative technical solutions that may be even better than what the officer had in mind. At the risk of sounding moralistic, let us nevertheless remember that procurement officers are not actually spending their own private money here. When they buy a kitchen for their own home, and with their own money, they are free to go to their favourite store and buy their favourite brand without comparing prices, if they like. But when spending public money, they must, as long as competitive procedures apply, give companies a chance to present their offers. This is even true when only a handful of companies have to be invited, for even then genuine competition must be ensured, and authorities must target firms that do sell what they want to buy. Besides, a procurement officer is anyway not necessarily in the best position to know what the latest technological developments in the market are. Procurement practice should in this sense be market-based, generating, at the very least, a sufficient number of tenders.[4]

So what just happened? What the procurement officer effectively did was to define *means*, not *ends*. He or she prescribed the solution – anti-theft gates with certain parameters – to achieve the underlying goal, which is to have alarms set off in case of attempted theft. Is it, however, really important to the contracting authority that the gates have a certain height or electromagnetic frequency? As long as the gates do not unduly hinder passage or disturb the functioning of the library, and as long as their frequency complies with health and safety standards, these specifications should be completely irrelevant. The only specification that actually does seem relevant is the detection range, i.e. how far down and how far up from the floor the system will detect a hidden book on a person walking through. As for the rest, it should be up to the economic operators to propose solutions. Maybe a company is selling gates that have a lower height but still have the same detection range, or that use a different but equally permissible frequency? There is no reason on the substance to exclude them from the award through needlessly narrow technical specifications. This point is especially pertinent since over-specification tends to work against small and medium-sized enterprises which otherwise could have pitched their alternative product.

Thus, in order to widen the field for competitors and to generate more choice for the contracting authority, the officer should reflect on what exactly his or her *needs* are, and draft the specifications accordingly. The end is, after all, to have a certain functionality, not a certain brand of gates as such: any proposed solution must ensure that an alarm is set off in case of a theft attempt, covering the library exit within such-and-such a range. And again, let us be realistic. It is rarely wise to try to be smarter than the private firms when it comes to innovative technical solutions. Communication between public procurers and bidders in award

---

4   PWC EU Services / Utrecht University, *Public procurement: Costs we pay for corruption*, 2013, p. 12.

procedures is generally more constrained and awkward compared with the frank discussions between buyers and sellers in the private sector.[5] But where open and transparent communication lines exist, notably in procedures with negotiation that can be available under national or EU procurement law, procurement officers should definitely explore how offers can match their specific needs.

3.2. MARKET RESEARCH

Even before publishing their call, i.e. at the preparatory stage, public buyers might decide to meet a number of potential suppliers to discuss what is currently available on the market. Not all market research is immediately a distortion of competition, and in fact the 2014 EU Public Procurement Directive explicitly envisages preliminary market consultations as a valid means to gather information.[6] This can be particularly instructive in cases where procedures with negotiation (after the opening of tenders) are unavailable, and the choice is effectively just between open and restricted procedures.[7] Nor should we actually be too afraid to use competitive dialogues, whereby authorities invite potential suppliers to discuss together what should go into the tender specifications, and how the call should be drafted, considering what is needed and what is available on the market.[8] True, competitive dialogue procedures are sometimes viewed critically because of their lengthiness, perceived lack of transparency and anti-competitiveness. And public buyers perhaps avoid them because they fear making mistakes, and do not wish to take the risk of having their award decision annulled in court. Indeed it seems that many procurers believe that competitive dialogues are only meant for buying space rockets, or satellites, or other hyper-complicated machines. In fact, already something relatively earthly as a canteen service can merit a competitive dialogue. Professional caterers will then be able to inform buyers frankly and openly of the latest innovations and possibilities when it comes to food choice, processing, supply policy, nutritional information, energy savings, staffing, pricing policies, and so on. Again, even with the most forward-thinking market research, the best solution may remain unnoticed until it is actually presented by a company. Conversely, it would be highly frustrating to sit and wait for offers in vain, simply because a certain clause or arrangement that we had foreseen turns out to be highly unusual in the market: something that is uneconomical from suppliers' point of view, that discourages companies

---

[5]   K. Lundvall, J. Tops & H. Ballebye Olesen, *What can public procurers learn from private?*, Copenhagen Economics 2008, p. 27.

[6]   Article 40 of Directive 2014/24/EU.

[7]   A.R. Apostol, 'Public procurement of innovation – A structural approach', *Public Procurement Law Review* (2012).

[8]   Article 30 of Directive 2014/24/EU.

from tendering, but that we could have easily avoided by talking to companies first.

3.3. VARIANTS

The above example of security gates for a public library can also illustrate another means to widen the field of competition: the admission of variants. Variants are solutions proposed by a tenderer which do not match the technical specifications of a call for tenders but which achieve the same result as the standard solution does. In essence, variants are a means for firms, especially innovators, to surprise a contracting authority with an alternative solution that the authority had not even thought of, and that can provide better value for money than conventional solutions. Under EU procurement law, a contracting authority may authorize variants irrespective of the award method: the 2014 Directive allows it for both price-quality ratio awards and lowest-bid awards.[9] Where variants are allowed, the contracting authority must state the minimum requirements that such variants must meet in order to be admitted to evaluation. If such minimum requirements are not fixed, variants are deemed not to be authorized.[10]

Practical examples could be technical variants or financial variants. For instance, where a contracting authority launches a call to replace old windows in an office building, and where that authority has authorized variants, a technical variant might instead propose a new technique of thermic insulation that keeps the old windows in place. To be admitted to evaluation, the variant would have to meet a more fundamental minimum requirement, which is to bring down heat loss through windows. In other words, the minimum requirement is that it achieves the defined ends. A financial variant would be an offer for a contracting authority to lease a car park, rather than to buy it; the minimum requirement is the making available of cars in one way or another.

The admission of variants can generate savings for the contracting authority. It does, however, require of procurement officers to think more thoroughly about what is actually needed. After all, it is not only necessary to define minimum requirements for variants, to make sure they are functionally equivalent to the model solution; it is also necessary, in the case of price-quality ratio awards, to formulate award criteria in such way that they are broadly applicable even to unexpected solutions. In the case of the replacement of windows, qualitative award criteria should then not focus on specifics like the thickness of the new windows or the material of the new frames, but rather on more fundamental considerations like energy savings over a certain period of time. In the case of

---

[9]   Article 45 of Directive 2014/24/EU.
[10]   See also case C-421/01 *Traunfellner*.

the acquisition of cars, operational and lifecycle cost and residual value but also administrative burden should play a role in the drafting of award criteria: a contracting authority that leases rather than outright owns its cars is free from the responsibilities of ownership, like having to take care of insurance or resale.

On the positive side, accepting variants *forces* us to think about the ends, rather than the means, which is something that we should be doing anyway. Returning to the example of security gates for the library, we have already established that it is not strictly necessary to prescribe the height and electromagnetic frequency of such gates, as long as they fulfil their function and comply with health and safety standards, and as long as a certain detection range is secured. But why, actually, insist on gates to begin with? What if there were a company that invented a new device to detect hidden books? And what if that device were not a gate at all, but a sensor attached to the ceiling, working not through electromagnetic frequencies but, say, ultrasound? The minimum requirement would be to have a system that triggers an alarm when someone tries to leave the library while hiding a book; the model solution would be conventional security gates; the award criteria would include reliability, visual intrusiveness and operational costs, which can be applied to any solution including pleasantly surprising ones.

It is perfectly understandable why contracting authorities tend to disallow variants. First, we almost have to predict what variant will arrive in order to draft our specifications accordingly. Second, allowing variants generally adds unpredictability to a procurement process where we are already happy if we get enough decent offers, make the award, and not receive any complaints. Perhaps this is the true value of the authorization of variants: they remind us to draft technical specifications and award criteria in such way that innovative solutions will not even count as variants, but just as possible solutions to match the need we have defined.

3.4. OPTIONS

Options denote elements of an order, described in a call for tenders, which the contracting authority may in the end decide to purchase or not. In the earlier example, security gates could be the main order while a device that keeps count of how many people pass through them could be optional. Another practical example could be the purchase of uniforms (main order) with or without coat hangers (option).

Theoretically a contracting authority may not yet know, at the time of the publication of the call, whether or not the option will be needed at the time of the award. Alternatively, the authority may not know whether it will be able to *afford* the options, given budget constraints, and so first has to see incoming offers. If there are funds left because the uniforms turn out to be cheaper than expected, for example, the authority may decide to order the hangers, too.

EU procurement law does not enter into much detail as to how options are to be defined and evaluated. The inclusion of options must be announced in advance; the only explicit requirement is that the value of options must form part of the overall value estimate.[11] Thus, in our example, if the estimated value of the uniforms is €50,000 and the estimated value of the optional hangers is €10,000, then the value that will determine whether the overall award reaches the threshold of the Directive or not is €60,000.

The main danger in the use of options presents itself where tenders are evaluated with options included, but where these options are then in fact not ordered; or where the evaluation is based only on the basic product but the options are then ordered nevertheless. In both cases we may find out in the end that, in fact, another company would have been cheaper or better than the one to which we have awarded the contract. Consider the following example with two tenderers, both offering a price for the basic product and a total price in case the option is ordered as well.

Figure 1. Distorted competition in case of evaluation with and without options

Tender	Basic price	Price including options
A	€5,000	€5,500
B	€4,500	€6,000

Let us assume that we award the contract to the lowest bidder. If we evaluate only the basic price, we would award the contract to B, but if we then also order the options from B, it turns out that A would have been cheaper and would have deserved the overall award. Conversely, if we evaluate the price including the price for the options, A is cheaper, but if we decide not to order the options, B would have been cheaper.

For this reason we generally recommend not to use options at all. In cases where it is unavoidable that the purchase of some elements is certain but the purchase of other elements is not, however, we suggest the following three approaches to at least minimize the risk of distorted competition. Each approach corresponds to a distinct type of options: (1) options which can be obtained separately from the main order; (2) options which are a feature of the main order and thus must be ordered as part of the main order and cannot be ordered separately; and (3) options which can be ordered later but which will then have to be provided by the same contractor.

---

[11]   Article 5 (1) of Directive 2014/24/EU.

3.4.1. DISSOCIATED OPTIONS

First, there are cases where the options can be bought separately from the main product. Let us call them dissociated options. Examples include the earlier uniforms, for which the coat hangers are options that could theoretically be supplied separately by the same company or by a different company. Such dissociated options are effectively lots, and for the purpose of clarity they should be named and treated as such. In general, lots are separate parts of an overall order that is split up so as to enhance competition, because then small or local or specialized firms can compete just for certain parts of the award. In the example, lot 1 would be the uniforms and lot 2 the hangers, and it is up to the contracting authority to decide whether to award one, both, or none. The evaluation for both lots would take place separately. In the example above, B would win lot 1 because its basic product alone is cheaper, while A would win lot 2 because A's price is lower for the separate optional part. Alternatively, the option could be simply quantitatively more units of the same item: for example 5,000 computers, with another 1,000 of the same type of computers as options. In that case, it might be a sensible choice to award a framework contract based on a unit price multiplied by the probable number of required units. Thus, the company with the best offer will commit itself to supply as many computers as are needed for the fixed unit price. If the needed units will have to be ordered in several big batches, another possibility is a framework contract with several contractors, whereby competitive offers are requested for each new order. Thus, for each batch of 400 computers, prices are requested, and the lowest bid for that shipment wins.

3.4.2. ASSOCIATED OPTIONS

The second type of options is associated options, meaning features that are part of the main object of a call for tenders that cannot be bought separately. An example would be air conditioning in a car: it either comes as an extra with the car, or it does not, but we cannot buy air conditioning alone. Presumably it is an option because we do not know whether we will be able to afford a car with air conditioning, since we have not seen the offered prices yet. In this case, we recommend carrying out a double evaluation. All tenders are first evaluated with the option included; if the best offer exceeds our available budget, we evaluate all tenders without the options, and see whether the best offer without the options stays below the ceiling. This applies to both lowest-bid awards, where only the price decides and the cheapest offer wins, and to awards based on who offers the best price-quality ratio. In both cases the winning offer can exceed our budget, and in both cases it would make sense to see who wins if the optional extras are removed. Of course, this double evaluation would have to be announced in advance in the tender documents, so that firms will know in what manner their tenders will be evaluated.

3.4.3. LOCK-IN OPTIONS

The third type of options is perhaps the most problematic. It concerns cases where the contracting authority cannot yet know, at the time of the award, whether an option will be needed in the end, but once the option becomes necessary, the order for the option can only be awarded to the firm that has already obtained the main contract. Let us call these lock-in options. An example may be renovation works, with the optional use at a later stage of a special paint by the same painting company; or a scientific study about five countries, with the optional possibility to later add two more countries to the same study. We will engage neither a new painting company nor a new researcher for the options: they will have to be executed by the already chosen contractor. Here there is no other way but to be honest and transparent about the uncertainty of whether or not the option will be needed. The tender documents should, for example, indicate as accurately and realistically as possible what the factors are that might determine whether the options are ordered or not: legislative reforms, external demands, the result of the execution of the main order, etc. This will not completely remove the uncertainty, but at least firms will be able to design better informed offers under more transparent tendering conditions. The evaluation should be carried out on the whole tenders including options, otherwise we risk allowing firms to charge us whatever they want for the options once they have won the main contract. If possible, though, the weight of the evaluation of the options should be adjusted to the probability of the order. In the example of special paint, if there is only a fifty-fifty chance that the special paint will be needed, the tenderers' price for it should be multiplied by 0.5. This way, the price of an option that is ordered only half the time will also have half the weight of the price of an order that is needed always. Otherwise, firms risk needlessly inflating their total price with prices for items whose necessity is less than certain.[12]

3.4.4. OBLIGATION TO TENDER FOR OPTIONS

Should all firms be obliged to make an offer for the options? This depends on whether the contracting authority needs to be certain that the contractor will be able to provide the option as well, or whether this is irrelevant. If orders are

---

[12] See Chapter 6 on price schedules for a detailed discussion on how quantities should be weighted and why.

basically separate lots, it should be up to the firms to decide whether they wish to compete for one, several, or all parts of the order. Perhaps a firm can supply coat hangers but not uniforms: let it make an offer just for the coat hangers then, and award the uniforms contract to someone else. The same logic holds true in case of double evaluation for associated lots, when we do not know whether our budget suffices to cover the options. If a firm can only offer cars without air conditioning, let it offer what it can offer: it will simply not compete in the first round, where only cars with air conditioning are evaluated, but might stand a chance in a possible second round. Only lock-in options should be mandatory: if we reserve the right to order something extra with the same contractor at a later stage, we must be sure that the contractor will be able to perform. In that case, all tenders should include prices and conditions for the option as well.

3.5. PARALLEL TENDERS

If the contracting authority awards a contract to the lowest bidder, tenderers will be interested in making their lowest price offer. If, however, the award goes to the tender that offers the best price-quality ratio, and if firms have several products that they can theoretically offer, tenderers will not know exactly whether they should offer basic quality at a low price, or better quality at a higher price. Perhaps the better quality will more than compensate for the higher price and win, but this is not certain.

In order to open up competition as widely as possible, and in order to be able to choose among the greatest number of possible solutions, the contracting authority should, when applying a price-quality award, consider allowing tenderers to make more than one offer. Using such parallel tendering, a firm can propose a cheap low-end solution *and* a more expensive solution of higher quality, and see which one is best suited to the needs of the contracting authority. Allowing parallel bids is an efficient way of boosting choice with the same number of competitors. It also frees firms from the need of otherwise having to ask sister companies or other fake competitors to bid in a different price range. To limit the administrative burden of evaluating *too many* offers, the authority may decide to limit the number of bids to, for example, two or three per firm.

CHAPTER 4

SELECTION CRITERIA

Selection in procurement law means the sifting of tendering firms based on their capacity to execute the contract. A contracting authority may state that, for example, for a certain works contract, only firms that have carried out similar works before may tender – the selection criterion in that case being sufficient professional experience. If after applying selection criteria we conclude that a firm does not have enough capacity, in this case experience, we will not even look at the content of its offer: it gets rejected. Selected firms, by contrast, move on to the next stage and have their offer evaluated on the substance.[1]

4.1. THE EU LEGAL FRAMEWORK

As regards EU member states, national rules determine whether and how firms' professional and financial capacity is verified. For awards with values above the EU thresholds, however, basic rules from EU legislation and case-law apply to the procurement process. The 2014 EU Public Procurement Directive defines three types of selection criteria:[2] (1) criteria relating to authorizations (whether firms possess the necessary licences to carry out the work in case of award); (2) criteria relating to economic and financial capacity (whether firms are financially robust enough to carry out the work in case of award); and (3) criteria relating to technical and professional capacity (whether firms are skilled, equipped and experienced enough to carry out the work in case of award). Evidently, selection criteria must be formulated in advance, so that firms will know on which basis their capacity will be assessed.[3] This is not only a transparency requirement for contracting authorities in its own right, to protect against abuse; it is also economically efficient, because firms which see that they do not meet the selection criteria anyway can save themselves the trouble of tendering.

---

1   If selection criteria are applied after the award criteria, as is allowed under Article 57 (2) of Directive 2014/24/EU, then the presumed winning tenderer is eliminated if it turns out that he or she has insufficient capacity under selection criteria.
2   Article 58 of Directive 2014/24/EU.
3   See cases C-470/99 *Universale-Bau*, C-368/10 *Commission v. Netherlands*, par. 107.

4.2. THE LOGIC OF SELECTION CRITERIA

It may very well be that, in practice, the choice of selection criteria, and the proofs requested to verify them, becomes something of a habit. For instance, it may become routine – and it has become routine in many European countries – to impose a minimum annual turnover as a financial selection criterion, or to request a list of firms' equipment as part of professional capacity assessment. We would like to recall, however, that the design of selection criteria and proofs should not be a mere routine, but a conscious choice to make sure that we do our best to avoid certain risks. For example, why do we ask for lists of equipment under professional selection criteria? Because we only want to deal with well-equipped firms. Why? Because giving the contract to an ill-equipped firm might lead to faults, delays, and budget overruns. Poor equipment may be a sign of insufficient professionalism. Are we ever going to reject a firm for insufficient equipment, though? Or for not having the "right" equipment, based on what *we* think is the right equipment? If not, perhaps it is enough for firms to show that have done similar works before. Then it is up to them to have or obtain the necessary tools.

Why do we ask for minimum turnover? Because turnover, meaning the amount of money a company has earned selling its goods or services (before subtracting its expenses, like salaries and taxes), indicates the volume of a company's activity and, basically, its sheer size. Why is that important? That depends on why it is important *to us*. Perhaps it is important to us because our contract requires investments on the part of the contractor, and we do not want the firm on the first day to come and ask for advance payment. Or perhaps a company may lack the necessary professional capacity to handle a contract that alone is worth as much as its total sales in a year. Thus, turnover becomes an indirect indicator of experience, or its ability to handle more than one client. If a company depends just on us for its survival, this may increase the risk that it will have trouble to continue working, to finance investments, and to pay its workers, in case of financial difficulties. For us this could mean aborted contract performance, delays, costs, or even the necessity to quickly find a new contractor.

The 2014 EU Public Procurement Directive rightly limits contracting authorities' freedom to request capacity proofs – forcing them to accept certain certificates, limiting the number of categories of proofs that can be demanded – since burdensome selection criteria and proofs tend to favour only the largest companies. Instead, the Directive relies on a much more market-based approach: while we can check firms' capacity based on selection criteria that are important to us, this selection may not be excessive, and should not lead to the needless elimination of perfectly fine companies, potentially to the benefit of a single company, possibly the company we had had in mind all along.

The design of selection criteria sometimes starts with the proofs that tenderers must submit. In fact, the definition of proofs is the *outcome* of a thinking process which is basically a risk assessment. The actual reasoning should start at the beginning: (1) what is the danger that we want to avoid (risk), (2) what is the capacity that firms must have in order to lower the risk (selection criteria), and (3) what are the means by which firms can show that they meet the selection criteria (proofs). For example:

Figure 2. The logic of the design of selection criteria and corresponding proofs

Risk We want to avoid: →	Selection criterion Therefore firms must be: →	Proofs Therefore firms must show us:
… that our contractor causes faults, delays, cost overruns	experienced	their list of references
	well-equipped	their list of tools
… that our contractor cannot handle the size of the contract	large	their annual turnover
… that our contractor goes bankrupt	financially healthy	their financial statements

If we want to avoid contracting a firm that is likely to go bankrupt within a year, then this is a legitimate concern. The corresponding selection criterion is financial health, since experience, equipment or size are not safeguards against bankruptcy. If the criterion is financial health, we must analyse firms' finances – chiefly the balance sheet and the profit-and-loss account – because lists of references or tools, or turnover alone, do not indicate financial health. Thus, whenever we insist on certain proofs, it should always be because we need these proofs in order to verify compliance with a certain selection criterion; and whenever we impose a certain selection criterion, it should be because we want to avoid a certain risk: a risk that is minimized if we decide to deal only with companies that fulfil that criterion. None of this will *guarantee* us that the risk will be completely gone: a financially healthy firm is one that has a low probability of bankruptcy, but it may nevertheless suddenly become bankrupt; an experienced firm is one that has carried out many similar contracts before, but it may nevertheless make mistakes or cause accidents. The point of imposing selection criteria is to do what is necessary and reasonably possible to lower a certain risk. If the risk is minimal to begin with – in case of a low-value, short-term service contract, for example – we might as well assume that, by tendering, firms imply that they have what it takes to carry out the task. Then there is no need to impose on them any administrative burdens in the form of proofs.

Let us not forget that the imposition of selection criteria is, necessarily, a restriction of competition. If we use them, then there will be firms that we may need to reject on these grounds, and there will be firms whose offer we will never see because, having read our criteria, they will not even bother to tender. The only question is whether this restriction of competition is justified or not. High-risk, high-value contracts may call for high standards at the selection stage. In markets where the presence of innovators drives quality, by contrast, we may easily risk choking competition if we are too strict: start-up companies will for example have difficulty complying with selection criteria that rely on past performance, such as turnover in previous years. In such cases we recommend leaving the door open for tenderers to prove their actual capacity *by other means*. Regarding turnover, a start-up may not have had several years of turnover yet, but might prove that it already has large clients and sound finances to support its activity.

And let us not forget either that selection criteria do not always have be announced in the form of thresholds to begin with: we may test a criterion such as "appropriate professional capacity in the light of the complexity and scope of the contract" in the form of an individual appraisal. True, stating that a firm must have done maintenance work either for one building of 40,000 m^2 or two buildings of 20,000 m^2 sounds very objective and mathematical, but we may thereby inadvertently exclude capable firms for no reason. In cases where we can tell whether a firm is serious without being able or willing to fix a quantitative threshold, a capacity scoring or, in case we limit the number of selectable candidates, a ranking, both duly explained and justified, may replace the automatism of threshold-based selection.

4.3. FINANCIAL CAPACITY

Financial capacity, or financial standing, refers to the economic situation of a company, which can be relevant as a selection criterion. In order to determine which financial indicators are relevant to a contract and which ones are not, let us first revisit a few basic principles of corporate accounting and the way they are relevant for procurement design.

4.3.1. ACCOUNTING PRINCIPLES

A common way to assess firms' economic and financial capacity is to review their two most important accounting documents: the profit-and-loss account and the balance sheet. The profit-and-loss account shows a company's performance based on the value entering and leaving it over a given period of time, for example one year. It starts with the turnover, meaning all the money the company has earned by selling its products; it lists how much the company has had to pay for raw materials, salaries, taxes and other costs; and, in the bottom line, it shows how much money the company had left in the end (if any). The balance sheet, by contrast, shows a company's financial situation at any given point in time, for example the end of the year. On the left, the balance sheet shows its assets, meaning everything that it has – buildings, machinery, the money that it has in its bank account. On the right are the company's liabilities, meaning the things that finance the assets and explain where these assets come from. If a company borrows one million euros from a bank over ten years, this will show up as one million euros of immediately available cash on the assets side, and as one million euros of long-term debt on the liabilities side. The sum of all assets must be equal to the sum of all liabilities, because the origin of all assets must be accounted for.

Figure 3. Simplified models of a profit and loss account and a balance sheet

Profit and loss account	Balance sheet	
Sales (turnover)	Assets	Liabilities
– expenses	• Buildings, machines	• Capital
– salaries	• Patents, licences	• Reserves
= Gross profit (EBITDA)	• Money invested	• Long-term debt
– amortization, depreciation of assets		
– interests paid	*Liquid assets:*	*Short-term debt:*
= Earnings before taxes	• Bills clients still need to pay	• Bills the firm still needs to pay
– taxes	• Cash	• Short-term bank loans
= Net earnings (profit or loss)		

4.3.2. TURNOVER

As noted, a typical selection criterion is that tenderers must have had a certain minimum annual turnover for a certain number of years. This is easy to find, it is the top line in the profit-and-loss account. Why is it relevant? Because turnover stands for size – and size in turn can indirectly also stand for other things, such as experience, reputation and general trustworthiness. It is absolutely legitimate, for example when awarding large-scale works contracts, to specify that companies should not be too small. In that case, to give a stark illustration, we do not want a one-man business to promise us to hire fifty engineers and buy twenty excavators if only it gets the contract: we want to deal with a company that is large already.

When fixing actual thresholds, we should always consider the proportion of *annual* turnover to the *annualized* contract value. If a one-year contract has a value of €1,000,000, then we might require firms to have an annual turnover twice that value, in this case €2,000,000. It means that, in essence, the firm will have one other client of the same size apart from us, or the sum of the values of all its other contracts is equal to the value of ours. The value of our contract must in any case be annualized if we wish to use it as a reference for turnover, because turnover is also annual. If not, then multi-annual contracts will inflate the importance of the selection criterion. If the contract lasts two years, and has a total value of €2,000,000, then we should not ask for an annual turnover of €4,000,000 because that needlessly excludes smaller firms. We should ask, if we want to keep proportions stable, again for a turnover of €2,000,000 since it is, annually, twice as much as the annualized contract value. Conversely, for contracts lasting much less than a year, requiring a turnover twice as high as the total value makes little sense either. If a contract is worth €100,000 but only lasts one month, then it would be unwise to ask for a minimum turnover of €200,000. After all, this would mean that the firm has one other client during that one month, but no clients at all for the other eleven months, or that our one-month contract alone has a value six times its normal monthly turnover. Again, it is annualized value that counts. The annualized value of our contract is, in this case, €1,200,000, so the minimum annual turnover, if we insist that it should be twice as much, should be €2,400,000.[4]

4.3.3. NET AND GROSS EARNINGS

Regrettably, sometimes it is required that tenderers must have had positive net earnings, or positive earnings before taxes, for a number of consecutive years. This is the bottom line in the profit-and-loss account, or the item just above the bottom line, respectively. Why is that relevant? We honestly do not know.

Profits rather than losses tell us nothing about a company's size, nor about its health, only about its profitability during a given year, but that alone does not say much. A firm with an annual turnover of 50 million euros could well generate profits in one year, and an exceptional €200,000 net loss in the next. For example, because there was a drop in turnover, due perhaps to an economic crisis or another factor, while salary costs and overheads stayed the same. Or because the company made large investments in machinery, which by itself is rather positive, but part of the amortization of the new equipment will nevertheless already show up as losses. Still, one way or another, the loss represents in this case 0.4%

---

[4]   Watch out, though, that you do not get a reputation for always automatically requiring a turnover that is twice the annualized contract value, because then the minimum turnover will always be an even number and reasonably smart tenderers will be able to deduct from that what your available budget is. Similarly, if you publish minimum turnover for each of twenty lots in a row, make sure you do not automatically multiply your estimated value by three either: if the sum of the digits in a figure can be divided by three (like 261,000), then the figure itself is a multiple of three as well. We recommend rounding off: downwards to enhance competition, upwards to decrease the risk of dealing with companies that are too small.

of its turnover, almost nothing, but the "profit" criterion would already have excluded the firm.

Conversely, a firm may well generate profits, but be so heavily indebted that it will be bankrupt within six months. Or its net earnings may be positive only because of financial and accounting operations that have nothing to do with its core business, such as gains from capital interests or intra-holding transfers made for tax purposes, gains from positive amortizations and capital appreciation, and the re-booking of earlier provisions. All these operations influence net earnings, but they do not truly reflect a company's activity. A provision is money reserved for expected future expenses, and if they turn out not to be necessary, the money becomes available again; amortizations and capital depreciation are fictitious losses, or earnings, that relate to the calculated value of a company's assets, but they do not represent any actual movement of money.

If anything, the most significant – or rather the least insignificant – indicator in this context is positive *gross* profits, meaning positive earnings before interests, taxes, depreciation and amortization, or EBITDA. It means having sold products, and deducted the cost of selling these products, the company has money left to pay for all the other items that come afterwards. Being at a loss even before taxes are paid is not a good sign. But even that may, for a single year, be explained. Therefore, positive EBITDA is less bad than positive net earnings, but it remains a single, isolated indicator, and is therefore a very crude indicator of financial health. Both can let unhealthy firms through, while excluding healthy ones, meaning that perfectly fine firms, having seen the criterion, will not even bother to tender.

4.3.4. ECONOMIC VIABILITY

When it comes to assessing a company's financial health, we recommend a financial analysis of its most recent balance sheets and profit-and-loss accounts, taking into consideration a number of ratios and other indicators to determine whether the company is at risk of going bankrupt. If a contracting authority does not have the means to carry out such an analysis itself, we recommend either contracting out this work to a nearby bank or rating agency, or using an automated financial analysis tool that is easy to use even for non-specialists: financial health scoring, which will be discussed below. Let us first revisit some basic notions of financial analysis, though.

To assess companies' health, financial analysts routinely use key figures from its accounting documents to see whether a certain figure is greater than another, or whether the ratio between one figure and another is higher or lower than what is desirable. For example, if there is too much short-term debt – meaning typically bank overdrafts and unpaid bills – and not enough quickly available cash, because all the assets are buildings and machines, it could mean that the company will have to start selling its machines to pay back its debt. The ratio of liquid assets to short-term debt should therefore, ideally, be greater than 1. The ratio between gross profit (from the profit-and-loss account) and total assets (from the balance sheet) is also interesting, because it shows whether the company succeeds in using its assets to generate cash. So is it a good sign if a company has lots of assets and no debt? Not necessarily: it could mean that the company is having trouble obtaining bank loans and thus cannot expand. Indeed, balanced long-term debt is generally considered desirable, also from shareholders' point of view, due to its leverage effect, meaning that the company can use the debt to acquire more assets and use those in turn to increase production, with added earnings ideally outweighing the cost of borrowing. Are net losses over two years in a row a problem? If the other indicators are robust, this may be just a temporary weakness that can be due to all kinds of factors. For example, large investments could have resulted in large amortizations, which show up as losses but are actually a sign of long-term thinking; a drop in demand during an economic crisis can diminish turnover, but not all costs can be reduced quite as quickly, for example personnel costs, yet if the company is well-financed in the long term, it should be able to absorb this temporary effect. Subsidiaries may be required to transfer their profits to their parent company, and this should be taken into account as well.[5] It may explain notably a small capital in comparison with turnover: if the parent company leaves all the losses with the subsidiary, but immediately pumps away all profits and pays them out as dividends to its shareholders, the subsidiary will be left with a heap of accumulated losses. Still, that subsidiary may be functioning normally and be perfectly viable for the rest. True, some key indicators allow us to make certain judgments on their own, but to make a more general assessment of financial health we have to look at several indicators in their mutual context.

Like we said, if we can do this ourselves, we should; if not, we can ask an external consultant to do it, or use a financial health scoring technique. To do this, all we need to do is ask tenderers to fill in an Excel sheet with a few key figures – this takes a company accountant three minutes – and calculate their score according to one of the methods described in the literature, notably the applicable Altman score or the Conan & Holder score. The formulas and further details are restated in Appendix I to this book. The scores translate the probability of a company's bankruptcy in the near future into a figure. They do that by considering different accounting indicators, and weighting them according to how big the impact of each indicator statistically is on the economic viability of companies in real life. The resulting figure, or score, can be in the "green" range, meaning that the company is healthy and the risk of bankruptcy is low. It can be in the "yellow" range, showing that there is some financial

---

5   See case C-218/11 *Edukövizig*.

imbalance. Or it can be in the "red" range, meaning that the company is on the brink of bankruptcy, that we should not award it any more contracts, and reject it at the selection stage.

If a company is "yellow", meaning neither clearly healthy nor clearly moribund, then it is up to us to decide what we will do. We could carry out an in-depth financial analysis – or hire a consultant to do this for us – to find the reasons for the imbalance, or let the company explain them to us, and then decide whether to reject or admit it. If the imbalance is due to the fact that the company systematically transfers all its profits to the parent company, or if the company was weak in the past but has just been acquired by a conglomerate so its future is safe, then we could simply insist on joint contractual liability of the parent company. If in-depth analysis is not possible, there is a more automated method, which is to specify that, in order to qualify, "yellow" cases must comply with *additional* criteria. We suggest that a company with a score in the "yellow" range should have had at least positive gross earnings (positive EBITDA) for the past two years, and positive net equity on the liabilities side of their balance sheet as of the end of the last year.[6] Net equity is the remaining value of a company that is left if it were to pay all its bills and sell all its assets: its capital and all the net earnings it has accumulated during its lifetime, which is also the most stable long-term source of financing for the company's activities. If there have been too many losses over the years, or the company has been excessively "drained" by its shareholders, net equity may turn negative so that it will need to borrow all its working capital through external financing and, after a possible liquidation, there will be nothing left, only debts. EBITDA should in principle be positive even during crises. Thus, imposing these two additional criteria on a company that is in the "yellow" area is an additional safeguard: if it fails these extra tests, it could be rejected. If the contracting authority considers, for a particularly sensitive contract, that a possible insolvency of a contractor is absolutely intolerable, it could also decide that "yellow" cases are rejected automatically. The price we pay is that we also reject firms that have a plausible explanation for their financial situation.

One way or another, our scoring method should be announced in advance. In addition, we should leave ourselves a clause saying that tenderers may nevertheless be rejected in case of doubts as to their real financial health. It may be, for example, that last year's annual report was still fine, but we know that the company has recently been convicted of some illegal activity, or lost a lawsuit over product liability, and the financial sanctions or the damage payments will possibly ruin the company, assuming that no provisions for these losses had been made on the balance sheet. In that case we need an escape clause, allowing us to reject tenderers with less-than-certain prospects of survival.

---

6   Here positive EBITDA is used as a criterion in context, as it should be, not as an isolated indicator.

4.3.5. INSURANCE

Article 58 (3) of the EU Public Procurement Directive 2014/24/EU proposes the use of professional risk insurance coverage as a financial selection criterion. The logic behind it is that, at least in certain sectors and circumstances, professional faults can endanger the performance capacity of a company. In an extreme case, an accidental death on a construction site, and the ensuing lawsuit, can ruin the company responsible for it: it will then not be able to pay us if it causes damage to us, and it will stop operations if it causes damage to a third party. Hence the wish for contractors to be covered. However, again, when insisting on insurance coverage, we need to keep in mind what exactly we try to prevent from happening, and what selection criterion we should impose as a result. Merely specifying that *some* insurance must be there is not a real criterion, because then indeed anyone with any type of insurance will qualify. Instead, the question is: what kind of risk must be covered by the insurance, and up to what amount? Works involving heavy machinery probably merit an insurance policy for corporeal and non-corporeal damage, so that the company will at least not go bankrupt in a serious case, and in these sectors professional risk insurance is often legally required anyway. A normal consultancy contract involves much less risk, and implies less of a need to verify insurance coverage, unless it is financial consultancy and we want the firm to have an insurer in case of wrongfully inadequate advice that causes us financial damage. Again, as with all selection criteria, proofs are there to show compliance with a criterion, which in turn is there to manage a certain risk. If we cannot really tell why we require certain proofs, then probably we do not actually need them.

4.3.6. OVERVIEW

Minimum annual turnover, in proportion to the annualized value of the contract, is useful for many contracts, namely where a contractor's size matters, but not for all, namely where it does not. Similarly, financial health is relevant for some contracts, but not for all. In one-off supplies contracts, for example, normally neither size nor financial viability are relevant. If we order a car and pay after delivery, the contractor's solvency is of little concern to us. If the firm goes bust before the car arrives, we do not pay; if it goes bust afterwards, we pay the liquidator and keep the car.

Figure 4. Typical financial selection criteria

Financial capacity requirement	Financial selection criterion	Possible uses	Idea to remember
Overall sufficient capacity, without specific details	Simple declaration by the tenderers that they have enough capacity	One-off supplies, payment after receipt, low-value contracts, generic contracts where it is easy to find a replacement contractor	"The company should have what is needed, and the risk if it does not is low or manageable."
Sufficient size, meaning indirectly enough staff, equipment, expertise, contacts, reputation, etc.	Minimum annual turnover	Contracts requiring investments on the part of the contractor, large and technically complex contracts	"I do not want to be the company's only client, nor its first large one."
Economic viability, low risk of insolvency in the near future	Good economic health score	Long-term contracts with mutual investments	"I do not want the company to go bankrupt while it works for me."

The above table gives a simplified overview of typical risks and the financial capacity criteria to address them. Evidently there are cases where entirely different solutions specific to the contract must be devised. For example, in a contract the object of which is to obtain insurance for government buildings, it is not so much turnover that is important to assess the capacity of an insurance company. It is rather the amount of reserves and its reinsurance coverage. Insurers generate turnover by selling policies, and to ask for a turnover even of several million euros would be completely ludicrous, when what actually matters is that there be billions upon billions of reserves and reinsurance coverage. This is merely a reminder that none of the possible financial selection criteria should be used by way of an automatism: they must be chosen and adapted to the risk we want to address and minimize for any given contract.

4.4. TECHNICAL CAPACITY

Technical and professional capacity is assessed in order to select tenderers that have, above all, enough equipment and enough experience for the contract. At least under the EU Public Procurement Directive, the number of types of proofs that can be demanded of firms is limited,[7] but actually the list is quite sufficient to verify capacity.

---

7   Article 60 of Directive 2014/24/EU.

For works and service contracts, but also for supplies, it is for instance typical to demand proof of experience in the form of a reference list, showing the main assignments performed and clients served in the recent past. This helps eliminate tenderers that are deemed too inexperienced for a complex contract. We should however stay realistic on what such reference lists can effectively prove. When we demand certificates of good execution of construction works, firms can very well choose to refer only to those contracts where the job was well done, and omit those where it was not. If contact details are requested and provided, these can be used to call previous clients and ask how things had really gone.

Some contracting authorities may be tempted to demand that only experienced staff should be working on its projects, and to therefore consider the training and professional experience of staff members under selection criteria. Apart from the possible overlap with qualitative award criteria, which we will discuss below, we advise against this for a very simple reason. Staff experience as a selection criterion is an indicator of the professionalism of the company *as a whole*: it is by itself no guarantee that the people whose CV we just read will actually be working on the project. We can ask for, and receive, the CV of a veteran team leader with an advanced engineering degree, but then this person is allocated to a different construction site, or becomes ill, or leaves the company, or retires, or becomes otherwise unavailable. We cannot, via selection criteria, plausibly require that all the best staff be pulled out from other projects and be allocated to our site, and that they never be allowed to change jobs. What we *can* do is conclude that the presence of certain experienced staff at a certain moment is an indicator of the company's overall professionalism, and select it on that ground. We thereby express our wish to only work with companies that have ten engineers *already*, rather than with companies that merely promise us to find and hire ten engineers if they get the contract. After that, any further requirements regarding the actual *commitment* of certain staff to a certain project, as part of the offer, should be fixed as a contractually enforceable minimum requirement in the technical specifications concerning contract performance, or as a qualitative award criterion.

Indeed, it is a particular phenomenon that professional selection criteria can overlap with qualitative award criteria. Yet selection and award criteria are, at least under EU law but also in their inherent logic, different concepts, even when both sets of criteria are applied simultaneously. Selection assesses the aptitude of the firm; award assesses the quality of its tender.[8] There have been cases of selection criteria that actually had nothing to do with a firm's capacity, and should instead have been award criteria;[9] conversely, there have been cases of

---

[8] See cases C-31/87 *Beentjes*, par. 16, T-387/08 *Evropaiki Dynamiki v. Commission*, par. 74.
[9] See case C-368/10 *Commission v. Netherlands*, par. 107. The case involved the fulfilment of "the criteria of sustainable purchasing and socially responsible business" and contributions to "improving the sustainability of the coffee market and to environmentally, socially and

award criteria that were actually selection criteria.[10] For a while there was some uncertainty in EU case-law about what to do with staff experience: on the one hand it is an indicator of a firm's professional capacity, on the other hand it may, notably in service contracts, also be an indicator of the quality of a tender.[11] The question has been settled by subsequent case-law[12] and the 2014 Public Procurement Directive,[13] clarifying that staff experience can also be an award criterion for contracts in which this has an impact on quality, but that there is still a difference between checking staff experience under selection criteria and considering them for the purpose of award criteria.

Thus, selection criteria concern the capacity of the tenderer. Apart from the examples already mentioned, such as a sufficient number of qualified staff, technical and professional selection criteria may include the requirement for firms to have enough branches in different cities, or enough excavators. So how can we tell they are not actually award criteria? It all depends on the purpose for which we request and consider certain information about firms. If we think that more excavators committed to a specific construction site mean better quality of performance, then this is an award criterion. If we think that not enough excavators in the firm's vehicle park means insufficient capacity, then it is a selection criterion. If below a minimum number of city branches we think that a firm will not be able to handle our contract, then this is a selection criterion; if we are willing to pay extra to have more branches, because it means extra service quality to us, then this is an award criterion. If we think that a firm with less than three senior structural engineers is not a serious firm, then this is a selection criterion; if we think that ten engineers committed to a project mean a higher-quality tender than five, or that engineers with twenty years of work experience add more quality to the tender than do engineers with ten years of work experience, then this is an award criterion.

What we should in any event not do is make the exact same thing a selection and an award criterion, thereby turning our assessment into a double check. Irrespective of whether it is legal or not, in purely practical terms the giving of quality points for professional capacity, which is already confirmed for everyone,

---

economically responsible coffee production". The other problem in this case was that the criterion was in any event too vague.

[10] See case C-315/01 *GAT*: the number of previous clients is an indicator of a firm's professional capacity, and therefore a selection criterion, not a quality criterion.

[11] While case-law such as T-4/01 *Renco*, par. 68, had accepted staff quality as an award criterion, C-532/06 *Lianakis* and subsequent cases C-199/07 *Commission v. Greece*, par. 55 and T-39/08 *Evropaiki Dynamiki v. Commission*, par. 39, declared unlawful a double-check of staff on both selection and award grounds.

[12] Cases T-447/10 *Evropaiki Dynamiki v. Court of Justice*, par. 42 and 53, T-457/07 *Evropaiki Dynamiki v. EFSA*, par. 75, T-32/08 *Evropaiki Dynamiki v. Commission*, par. 64.

[13] Articles 58 (4) of Directive 2014/24/EU on staff qualification as a selection criterion, and Article 67 (2) (b) on the qualification of assigned staff as a quality criterion in tenders where skills have an impact on tender quality.

means giving quality points for free. The result is that we needlessly neutralize quality differences between tenderers, so only the price is left to decide, and the cheapest offer wins. To avoid this trap, it is important to remember *why* we verify proofs under different criteria. Selection is there to reject firms that do not have the necessary means for the contract, and that are therefore inadmissible, while award is there to choose which tender is the best among those that in fact *are* admissible.

4.5. CONSORTIA

Sometimes firms team up to submit a joint tender as a consortium. The most blatant mistake for a contracting authority would then be to expect each and every member of a consortium to meet all selection criteria. After all, they probably do *not* meet all selection criteria on their own: if they did, they would not have needed to form a consortium. The point of a consortium is to pool resources, so that together the members have enough capacity.[14]

4.5.1. THE PROFESSIONAL CAPACITY OF CONSORTIA

As regards professional capacity, a painting company that is part of a consortium, for example, may not be able to show that it has done the electrical wiring in at least two buildings of similar size compared to the one where the works are to take place. That is because it only does the painting after the electrical works are finished. Relevant wiring experience should instead be proven by the consortium member that will in fact be responsible for the wiring. What consortia would need to show, however, is their plan how exactly they intend to divide tasks between their members. This will in turn allow the contracting authority to apply selection criteria to consortium members in proportion to their share, and thus to the consortium as a whole. A similar logic applies to the manufacturer of office furniture, the haulage firm that transports it, and the company that installs it.

4.5.2. THE FINANCIAL CAPACITY OF CONSORTIA

Technical selection criteria can however be easier to split up between consortium members than financial selection criteria. What if the financial selection criterion was a minimum turnover, or general financial health assessed by, for

---

14   See cases C-176/98 *Holst Italia*, C-218/11 *Edukövizig.*

example, an economic viability score? Should all individual consortium members meet each of these criteria on their own?

Again, it is the risk that counts. If firms should basically have a large enough size, because otherwise the contracting authority feels uncomfortable awarding the contract to them, then turnover can indeed be a much more meaningful indicator of size than, say, the number of employees. In that case, it would, regarding consortia, make sense to assess the turnover of each member in proportion to the value of the task assigned to it. It could be that, of a construction contract that is worth €50,000,000 per year, the plumbing has a value of €1,000,000 per year, and that tenderers must have an annual turnover twice the annualized value of the contract. Then, in case of a consortium, the firm that does only the plumbing should have an annual turnover of at least €2,000,000.[15] The logic is the same as if we had divided the contract into separate lots, each lot requiring different sorts of capacity. In fact, if we realize that our contract might be suitable for consortia, we should consider whether it might not make sense to actually divide it into lots in the first place.

Requiring each and every member of a consortium to have the minimum turnover for the whole contract strongly favours consortia between a few very large enterprises, and excludes consortia between larger and smaller firms. Requiring the minimum turnover as an *average* turnover for all consortium members would, however, be just bizarre. It would mean that all consortia would need to have a giant lead member to help raise the average of the smaller partners, but this is a mathematical exercise that has nothing to do with reality and companies' actual capacity. Again, we recommend applying thresholds in proportion to a member's share in the project.

What about overall financial health scores? These are used to assess the risk of future insolvency, rather than size. It may well be that the insolvency of even one consortium member will disrupt the overall contract performance to such an extent that the contracting authority can legitimately require all members to be in good health. By contrast, it may be that a member's bankruptcy will not matter too much. For example, it may be that the greatest value of a works contract lies in the raw construction, and if towards the end the painter goes bust, another firm can quickly be subcontracted to just finish the paint job. Thus, a contracting authority might require good health scores for all members executing a certain percentage of the overall task, and, if need may be, demand a plausible backup plan if one consortium participant, minor or otherwise, becomes unavailable.

---

15   Again, it is important to calculate turnover as a proportion to the *annualized* contract value, since turnover is also annual. Otherwise, contracts that last several years will inflate the minimum annual turnover requirement, while annual turnover in relation to the total value of a contract that lasts only a few weeks does not represent any real capacity.

In any case we do *not* recommend calculating a consolidated financial health score for the consortium, with members supplying their financial indicators that results in a global score as if the consortium were a company on its own. The fact is that, unless a new entity has been created, a consortium is *not* a company. The members retain their own capital, their own management, and they can go bankrupt individually. Joint and several liability means we can go after the surviving members for unpaid bills, but this does not help us if the crane operator went bankrupt so that for several weeks the whole construction site is on hold. If it is actually the case that a new company has been created by several firms, we should still consider the financial health of the founding members. The reason is that a fresh company has no past performance record that we can analyse, only its founding capital.

4.6. SUBCONTRACTORS

Subcontracting follows largely the same logic as the creation of a consortium: it allows tenderers to supplement professional capacity that they are missing by cooperating with another firm. Thus, if awarded the contract, the successful tenderer concludes a contract with another firm to have it carry out some of its assigned tasks.

One of the paradoxes of some procurement regimes or practices is that they impose different standards on consortium partners and subcontractors. Oddly, these regimes tend to be more lenient on subcontractors and more demanding towards consortium partners. Yet with consortium partners at least a direct contractual relation and a joint and several liability exists. With subcontractors it is much more important to avoid a case where one company wins the award but another does all the work while potentially evading conditions that would have applied, and would have been more diligently enforced, had it been a tenderer in its own right. We are not even speaking of subcontractors potentially breaching labour law standards on construction sites, but more basically about exclusion and selection criteria that are evaded simply because the firm is technically not the tenderer. In the case of exclusion criteria, imagine a company that has received a sanction for corruption or fraud, that asks a clean front company to tender, and that then takes over the awarded contract as a subcontractor. In the case of selection criteria, it may be that the contractor is more risk tolerant than the contracting authority is, subcontracting assignments to companies with levels of financial and professional capacity that would have been insufficient to pass selection criteria for tenderers. Even if the main contractor is contractually responsible for good and timely performance, and thus for a prudent choice of subcontractors, any damages may not compensate us for the real inconvenience of mistakes and delays, which can include not merely monetary but also reputational costs and political fallout.

To create fair tendering conditions, we advocate treating subcontractors analogously to partners in a consortium and the lead tenderers themselves, for example by specifying a percentage of subcontracted work above which subcontractors must submit the same proofs – via the tenderer – as the tendering company itself. Another way of limiting the risks of subcontracting is to anyway make subcontracting subject to prior approval, and to specify that certain core tasks of the contract cannot be subcontracted at all. Say we want, again, electrical wiring to be done: in that case it is legitimate to say that the winning company should do the wiring itself, instead of passing on the job to another company. The paint job after the wiring, since it is not the core of the contract but merely ancillary, may well be given to an approved subcontractor. In general, if tasks must be split between firms, a ban on subcontracting for core tasks instead promotes the formation of consortia, so again a direct contractual link with the executing firms will exist.

4.7. FAVOURING THE USUAL SUSPECTS

Without selection criteria we risk awarding contracts to firms that are, in short, not sufficiently serious. Yet when piling up selection criteria, another risk emerges, which is the needless exclusion of companies that would have had enough capacity for the contract. A similar risk is linked to the insistence on excessive volumes of paperwork to *prove* compliance with selection criteria, which favours big companies that have a whole department of tender drafters and lawyers and secretaries to take care of just that. This is why selection criteria must be appropriate to address an identified risk and be proportionate to that risk.[16] They must also be non-discriminatory. Does that mean that we cannot reject anyone? No, it means that selection criteria must not be designed in such way as to favour only specific companies without any proper justification. Selection criteria are *always* discriminatory, in a neutral sense of the word, because they discriminate against companies that do not meet them. The important thing is that this discrimination be objectively justified. The rejection of a firm is not a pleasant experience, but what is worse is the admission of firms that lack the minimum capacity as we had described it in the call for tenders. In that case our main concern should not be the well-being of that particular firm – which saw the selection criteria, knew that it was not admissible and tendered anyway – but the well-being of those firms that, having seen the selection criteria, were honest enough not to tender at all.

Regarding the assessment of selection proofs, we stress that capacity is checked by applying selection criteria to tenderers at the time when they tender. It may well be that, *at the moment*, a firm does not have quite enough special

---

16   Article 58 (1) of Directive 2014/24/EU.

excavators, but that they will be easily obtained in case it is awarded the contract. Financial capacity, the size of the existing vehicle fleet, or a draft purchase or leasing agreement with a manufacturer of excavators can all be indicative of a firm's willingness and ability to get the necessary tools in time. For yet again, selection criteria have to match the risk. On the one hand, we do not necessarily want to award a large building contract to a small start-up firm. On the other hand, we should not eliminate firms that can plausibly demonstrate that they have the means to have everything ready when the contract performance is to start. Define your selection criteria too narrowly, set the demands too high, and you might in fact end up favouring your current contractor company that already has all it needs because it already works for you.[17] This can anyway be illegal, but more generally it means lost opportunity to open up a market and invite better quality, better prices, or both.

---

[17]   See the reasoning in T-148/04 *TQ3 Travel Solutions*, par. 90, stressing the obligation of tenderers to have the necessary means for contract performance at the start of the performance, rather than at the moment they submit their tender.

CHAPTER 5

AWARD METHODS

After sifting tenderers for their compliance with, above all, exclusion and selection criteria, and after checking which tenders comply with the technical specifications, the contracting authority goes on to apply award criteria to the tenders found admissible. This is done in order to determine which bid should win on the substance, and which firm should actually receive the contract. In open procedures under the 2014 EU Public Procurement Directive, contracting authorities have the choice to first apply award criteria and only then verify whether the presumed winner also meets the exclusion and selection criteria.[1] In cases where the application of award criteria is straightforward – for example where only the price decides – while capacity verification is tedious, procurement officers can thereby avoid having to go through selection proofs of firms that would not win anyway. However, even when the order of verification of criteria is reversed, and full verification is carried out only for the presumed winner, any successful bidder must in the end still meet all cumulative criteria. And so we now turn to award criteria.

5.1. SINGLE AND MULTIPLE AWARD CRITERIA

Under the 2014 EU Public Procurement Directive, contracts are by definition awarded to the tender that is economically the most advantageous. Depending on the choice of the contracting authority, this can either mean the tender that offers the lowest price, or the one that offers a solution which entails the lowest overall cost, or the one that offers most value for money based on its price-quality ratio.[2] The most basic difference between these award methods is their number of award criteria. In lowest-price awards, there is only one award criterion, namely the price. This is why it is also called a price auction. Thus, once tenders are confirmed as being admissible, the only relevant difference between them is their price. The same holds true for lowest-cost awards, where the sole award criterion is the cost. Cost is the expense for the buyer in relation to a product, which includes the purchase price but also other expenses, such as

---

1   Article 56 (2) of Directive 2014/24/EU.
2   Article 67 of Directive 2014/24/EU.

storage, maintenance and disposal, and which can also differ between proposed solutions. Tenderers can be made to compete exclusively on the overall cost their solution generates. In price-quality awards, however, there is by definition more than one award criterion, because the contracting authority considers not only the price but also at least one quality aspect that is offered for that price. For example, a contracting authority may be willing to pay a basic price for a normal chair, but accepts paying extra for a leather chair. Thus, the two award criteria are "price" and "leather". A firm selling only leather chairs, which could not have competed on price alone because its products are more expensive than chairs made of fabric, may nevertheless offer a leather chair, and thereby compete on a combination of price *and* quality. Similarly, a firm selling only normal chairs is still in the race as well: had leather been a minimum requirement applicable to all offers, rather than an award criterion on which tenderers can compete, it could not have tendered to begin with.

Essentially, by choosing a lowest-price award, the message we send to firms is that we have clearly defined what we need, and that we will not tolerate any extra cost even if the proposed quality is higher than what we need. Firms are welcome to offer high-quality products, but the moment their model is more expensive than a simpler model, we will buy the simpler model. The message of a price-quality award, by contrast, is that firms can dare to propose quality that goes beyond minimum requirements, because added quality will be appreciated and will compensate a higher price. Just how much more we are willing to pay for more quality is expressed in the weighting of our award criteria. If our weighting is 90:10 in favour of the price, we are almost back in a price auction because the price will determine 90% of our decision, so firms should not try to charge us too much extra for their added quality. The lighter the relative weight of the price criterion becomes, the less the price tag matters to us, and the more boldly firms can try and distinguish themselves with their better quality.

5.2. LOWEST PRICE

Generally, an award to the lowest bid based on the price is, at least at the evaluation stage, the easiest method from an administrative point of view. It makes sense in the case of simple, generic purchases with clearly defined quality parameters. Let us say that we need a supply of light bulbs which are specific to the lamps we have in our buildings: only one particular type of light bulb will fit. Thus, we may publish a call to see which firm will supply these specific bulbs at the lowest price. Tenders offering a technically compliant product will have their price reviewed, and we will know immediately who has won. This is why lowest-price awards are also known as automatic awards.

Price is not the same as cost, though, because some things may be cheap to buy but cost more in the long run. If that is the case, it makes more sense to award the contract based on the lowest cost, instead of the lowest price. However, if the costs will be more or less the same no matter who gets the contract, then there is no point calculating them, at least not for the purposes of the call for tenders. We can then safely award on price alone.

Does quality play no role in lowest-price awards? It does, it is just that the minimum required quality is already exhaustively pre-defined in the call for tenders to begin with. This means that, from a quality point of view, tenders can be either technically compliant or not;[3] once their quality complies with our standards, the price decides the rest. This also means that we will not be able to buy quality that goes beyond our minimum requirements, at least not if it is more expensive. For example, some light bulbs may emit an even more pleasant light than we had required; but if they cost more than a cheaper model, under a lowest-price award we will have to buy the cheaper model. Thus, if we know exactly what we want, and refuse to pay more on extras, then the lowest-price award is absolutely appropriate. If, by contrast, we have a minimum requirement and are willing to spend extra for quality that is even better than that, for example a more pleasant light or a more customer-friendly after-sales service, then we should rather go for a price-quality award.

5.3. LOWEST COST

To stay with the example of light bulbs, it may be that several types of light bulbs will fit into the existing lamps. Some bulbs may come cheaply, others may be more expensive to buy but last longer and save electricity. This would be an ideal case to award the contract on the basis of the lowest cost, rather than the lowest price alone. The cost could be calculated based on, for example, the purchase price, multiplied by the number of times a bulb would have to be replaced over a number of years, plus the electricity spending over that number of years. This gives a more accurate impression of the true cost of a product, and allows us to save money in the long run.

Even before the entry into force of the 2014 EU Public Procurement Directive, costing had been a permissible method of calculating the true price under EU procurement law.[4] Since 2014, costing is explicitly authorized for high-value awards governed by EU law, covering both direct and indirect lifecycle costs for the buyer as well as external costs, such as environmental pollution.[5] In some cases the method of calculating costs, including external costs, is pre-defined

---

3   See case T-407/07 *CMB Maschinenbau*.
4   See case C-19/00 *SIAC Constructions*.
5   Article 68 of Directive 2014/24/EU.

because it is regulated by law, such as may be the case for motor vehicles.[6] In other cases the contracting authority will have to apply its own costing model, which then must equally be objective, verifiable, and accessible to all tenderers. Costs relating to acquisition can include switching costs, meaning the cost of installing new infrastructure to accommodate new equipment; operational costs include the consumption of resources as well as maintenance; end-of-life costs include, for example, disposal and recycling, or the resale revenues net of the administrative costs of selling, which do arise if we buy, and which do not if we lease. Where cost items can be specified by tenderers themselves, they can be requested as part of the price schedule. Where it is up to us to factor in certain types of costs, depending on what type of product is offered, we can add these costs to the price ourselves, as long as we have announced beforehand what we would do and how.

We are aware of the fact that a lowest-cost award takes more effort than a lowest-price award. We recall, however, that costs will have to be paid one way or the other. The only question is whether we want to take them into account already at the tendering stage or not. If costs play no role, or are by definition the same for all tenderers, then we can leave them out altogether. For example, if we award a simple services contract, or a contract for well-defined works, then the administrative and other costs will very likely be identical no matter who carries out the contract. In that case, cost is not subject to competition, so there is little reason to calculate it, at least for the purposes of the award decision. If costs can differ between possible contractors, though – and this is typically, though not exclusively, the case in supplies – then tenderers may be asked to compete on cost as well. It allows cost-efficient firms to use their competitive advantage in a way that they could not in a price-only award. We profit from such a cost competition because we simply pay less in the long run than we otherwise might.

5.4. PRICE-QUALITY RATIO

And then there are contracts whose object is not generic at all, so price or cost alone are not the only decisive factor. To stay in the theme of light bulbs, we may for instance decide to engage a consultancy firm to help us find savings to cut our electricity bill, for example by optimizing the occupancy schedule of our buildings. This is a service contract that should not necessarily go to the lowest bidder, but to the one whose expertise and methodology offers most value for money. This is exactly where not the price or cost alone, but the ratio between price and quality should decide. One consultancy may be more expensive than the other, but if the extra price is more than compensated by extra quality, it would deserve the award.

---

6   See Directive 2009/33/EC.

Essentially, the price-quality award method enables us to accept a higher price in order to obtain a higher quality. This is something that we cannot do under lowest-bid awards, because there we have to reject higher-quality offers the moment they start to cost more than the cheapest solution. Thus, if we are openly willing to spend extra on better quality, and if we want to incentivize firms to offer good value for money, and not just to be the cheapest among those complying with the tender specifications, then this calls for a price-quality award. Even for light bulbs, we may be willing to spend a little extra if their light is more pleasant, or if they reach full luminosity faster after switching on, or if the supply comes with a service that we appreciate, for example the possibility to order the bulbs online, to order them in smaller quantities with faster delivery so we can avoid large stocks in our own buildings, or to have them delivered to individual offices rather than to the central depot. In each case, increased quality – meaning quality that exceeds minimum standards – may well be worth paying for.

5.5. ELECTRONIC AUCTIONS

The EU Public Procurement Directive explicitly provides for the possibility of electronic auctions.[7] These are not actual award methods in their own right, but rather procedures that allow firms, once their tenders have been declared admissible and their technical content and quality has been evaluated, to lower their prices in one or several bidding rounds. Auctions can apply under all three award methods discussed. If the sole award criterion is the price, an electronic auction is an efficient form of continued price bargaining to bring prices down even further between the opening of initial tenders and the final award. If the award criterion is cost, the overall costs such as lifecycle costs can be determined at the beginning of the auction, and tenderers can then continue to compete on the purchase price. If the award goes to the best price-quality ratio, the offered quality can also be evaluated at the beginning, and tenderers can be invited to bring their price down: the lower the price at stable quality, the better the ratio.

There are a few caveats that we should add regarding electronic auctions. First, its use requires investment in an e-tendering platform with an auction function, ensuring a simultaneous auction closure, a possibility to track what the currently best offer is, etc. Second, electronic price auctions are useless where competition is weak and the risk of collusion between dominant companies is high. Third, electronic auctions – in fact any form of competition on price alone – can be economically inefficient where the quality aspect is of significance. After all, a price auction may incite tenderers to narrow their profit margins so much that the initially promised quality becomes unsustainable in the long run,

---

7   Article 35 of Directive 2014/24/EU.

or that employees will be paid below minimum wages. Price wars can even end in a sale at a loss to the contractor, which is often illegal under competition law. This is not to say that price auctions automatically or even frequently result in price dumping, but if the risk exists in a certain market already, multiple-round auctions may only stoke it further. In markets characterized by near-perfect competition and simple pricing, by contrast, such as commodities like electricity, paper or simple services based on unit prices, an electronic auction may lead to substantial economies compared with regular procedures with immediate awards.

5.6. NEGOTIATIONS

After the opening of tenders, negotiation, where available, can further improve the match between supply and demand. The 2014 EU Public Procurement Directive greatly expands the availability of negotiated procedures even for high-value awards,[8] making them more regular and less exceptional.

Where procurement procedures allowing for negotiations are available, we recommend using them widely. From the seller's point of view, a tenderer might otherwise make an initial offer, expecting negotiations and fine-tuning afterwards, and actually be surprised if the contracting authority immediately takes the first acceptable offer submitted, no questions asked.[9] From the buyer's point of view, forgoing negotiations potentially means losing an opportunity to obtain the same quality at a better price, or, more realistically, a higher quality for the same price, or a lower price after removing unnecessary quality features. And sometimes negotiations can simply be an efficient means to correct false impressions in case tenderers had misunderstood, when drawing up their offer, the description of our needs.

What should negotiation look like? There are practical questions whether we negotiate in writing or (ideally after having followed a professional training) in person, with all candidates present or separately with each of them, in one round or several rounds. Yet these are above all questions of individual preferences, internal policy, the number of tenderers and the nature of the contract. More fundamentally, however, we need in any case to be aware of our own preferences and the environment in which we negotiate, because this will determine the object of negotiation to begin with. In economic sectors where cost structures differ between companies and profit margins are high, it may certainly be

---

[8]   Article 24 (4) of Directive 2014/24/EU.

[9]   Article 29 (4) of Directive 2014/24/EU on competitive procedures with negotiation in fact provides that immediate awards based on initial offers and without negotiation are only possible when the contracting authority had specifically indicated that it might use this option.

efficient to seek a reduction of the price while keeping the same quality. In the case of contracts where the price is mostly determined by the wholesale price of supplies or by labour costs, and where profit margins are narrow, it is much more sensible to consider quality as the most important variable. Negotiations are more common in some sectors than in others; and it surely matters whether we are a central purchasing body dealing with medium-sized firms or a single local authority dealing with multinationals. In either case, where negotiations take place, the objective is not to corner the firms or ourselves, but to give and take and reach a new equilibrium.[10]

As regards the price, if we award the contract to the lowest bidder whereas the technical specifications are already fixed, we should identify for ourselves a target price that we consider appropriate for the quality we seek, an upper threshold price that should make us start negotiations, and a reservation price above which we will find prices unacceptable.

Figure 5. Possible price ranges and thresholds triggering negotiations

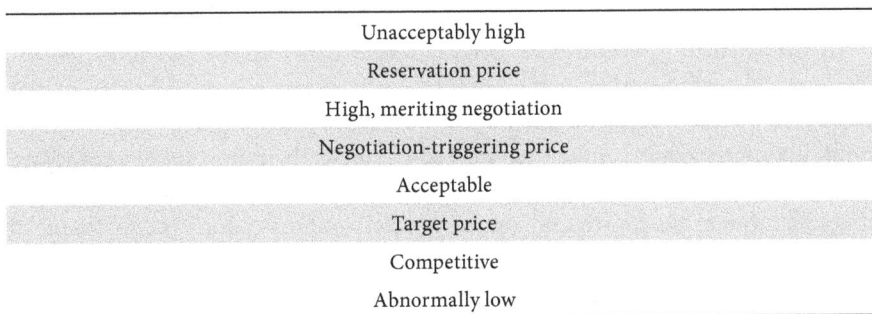

Unacceptably high
Reservation price
High, meriting negotiation
Negotiation-triggering price
Acceptable
Target price
Competitive
Abnormally low

Defining a negotiation-triggering price even before the opening of tenders allows us to swiftly decide whether possible savings will justify the cost of bargaining. Defining a reservation price before entering negotiations allows us to pursue negotiations with the clear condition that, above a certain price, we are willing to "walk away" from the contract, meaning to cancel the call for tenders if no-one else offers a lower price. If an agreement is reached on a price axis, however, it will necessarily be located between the seller's reservation price and ours. Normally reservation prices are not disclosed in negotiations, unless the reservation price is credibly imposed from above as a form of hand-tying ("I am sorry but we are not allowed to pay more than so-and-so much for a service vehicle", or, from the seller's point of view "I am sorry but the parent company does not allow me to give any rebates").

---

10   See also W. Lawther, 'Contract Negotiations', in K. Thai, ed., *International Handbook of Public Procurement*, Boca Raton: CRC Press 2009.

If we award the contract to the offer with the best price-quality ratio, we should equally determine an acceptable ratio, a lower, negotiation-triggering one, and a reservation ratio below which we find a tender unacceptable. If the price is a suitable variable while quality, once proposed, is constant, lowering the price will result in a higher price-quality ratio. The best quality that we are willing to pay for may, for example, score 100 quality points, but even for that we would be willing to pay at most €50. Our reservation ratio – quality divided by price – is therefore 2 quality per euro.[11] If, at 100 total quality, the price offer is €55, it means that, at a ratio of 1.82, the tenderer is trying to overcharge us for the proposed quality. If, as before, the variable is the price, the tenderer should decrease it to restore a ratio of 2. Alternatively, if quality is a variable as well, the tenderer could lower the quality slightly while offering a big rebate: after all, if the quality drops from 100 to 90 while the price drops from €55 to €45, the ratio will again be an acceptable 2 per euro. Where quality is below the maximum at the start, subsequent increases in quality will further improve the price-quality ratio if the price remains stable or if it increases less significantly than quality does.

In the spirit of give-and-take, what is it that firms hope to obtain *from us*? The most immediate value of the contract to tenderers is evidently the money, which will generate turnover and, if the earnings are higher than expenses, net profit. But there is more. A contract may be strategically important to a company. Companies that are nearly bankrupt will offer even extremely, unsustainably low prices just to win the award and stay alive a little more – which is why financial health can be an important selection criterion for long-term contracts.[12] More commonly, a company might expect that, once it is the incumbent contractor for one authority, it will find it easier to attract future contracts from the same or neighbouring authorities. If our contract allows the company to expand, it might be capable to seek even bigger contracts in the future and generate even higher turnover and, ideally, even larger profits. And there are reputational advantages: we might offer the company the permission to use our contract, our reference as a client, or our positive testimony, in its advertisement. This costs us nothing, but can be of great value to the firm. Which is a logic that lies at the very heart of market transactions: the item that is sold is of higher value, meaning of higher utility, to the buyer than it is to the seller. It is the same logic that allows us to drop quality features that are expensive but not very useful to us, in order to reduce the price, or to accept higher prices for things that we appreciate more than they cost in money terms.

How far can negotiations, especially alterations of technical specifications, go before they turn into an illegal collusion to agree on new terms outside proper competition? Different countries and authorities have their own regulations and

---

[11] See Chapter 9 regarding the calculation of quality-price ratios.
[12] See Chapter 4.3 on financial selection criteria.

guidelines. As a matter of principle, we suggest a "substantial modification" test by analogy to EU procurement law concerning modifications to already awarded contracts.[13] The question is whether the altered technical terms would have allowed other companies to participate in the tendering procedure had they been known to them beforehand. Obviously there will never be absolute certainty, but we can use our reasonable judgment: companies that can supply security gates can be expected to be able to provide them with or without an alarm counter. This is why changing secondary features of a basic product should be legitimate. Meanwhile, the acceptance of a generic solution, instead of the initially described specific solution, would be unfair, if there may have been companies that could have offered a generic solution from the start but, under the initial terms, could or did not tender. Simple metal detectors are, for example, more widely available than specialized devices detecting explosives or hazardous materials. If we had published a call to obtain the latter but, after negotiations, after all decide for the former, then we will have bypassed fair competition. In the highly exceptional cases where changes to technical specifications take us so far that we are essentially preparing an entirely different award, the only solution is to cancel and relaunch the call under new conditions. If, in fact, it may be *expected* that negotiations will take us very far from the initial descriptions, this should compel us to conduct deeper market research before publishing the call, or to launch a competitive dialogue,[14] or a comparable procedure, if available, where the content of tender specifications is discussed with potential tenderers as part of the procedure itself.

5.7. THE PROS AND CONS OF DIFFERENT AWARD METHODS

Price-quality ratio awards in general are sensible choices because their logic probably comes closest to the normal purchases we make in everyday life. This brand of milk is cheaper, but that one has a bio label; this chair is more expensive, but it is made of leather and the other one is not; the business class seat on the airplane costs more, but the comfort is higher; the comfort may be higher, but is it really worth the higher price, especially on a short flight? The answers in each case depend on individual preferences. We are ready to pay higher prices on quality traits that we find important. Conversely, we are unwilling to pay more for things that we do not really care about, or for things that we consider basic and self-evident. Sometimes we know what we need, and really just go for the cheapest product that fits the bill, which is the equivalent of lowest-price awards. But often we only know more or less what we need, we are willing to consider

---

13   Case C-454/06 *Pressetext* and Article 72 of Directive 2014/24/EU.
14   Article 30 of Directive 2014/24/EU.

different quality ranges and see whether, in our view, higher prices are justified or not. This is precisely the logic of awards based on the best price-quality ratio.

It is tempting to think that lowest-bid awards are most suited for public buying because they are so very objective: after all, the contract is awarded to the tenderer whose price is objectively the lowest. We have strong doubts about such a presumption of objectivity. This is because the award goes to the lowest bid *that meets technical requirements,* and these technical requirements are still written by the contracting authority itself. If it wants to buy, say, cheap and simple mobile phones for the use as service phones, then it can write very simple technical specifications and buy the cheapest models on the market. If it wants to buy expensive phones, it can write very demanding specifications from the start, and buy itself expensive phones. More precisely, it will buy the cheapest model, but from among high-end brands. Even things made of solid gold, and encrusted with diamonds, can be bought in a lowest-bid award, as long as we specify that any technically compliant product must be made of solid gold and include diamonds.

Awards based on price-quality ratio, meanwhile, equally contain a subjective element, because, as always, the contracting authority defines what it subjectively is willing to pay for. And, as always, minimum technical requirements are also set in advance. But here everyone will have to compete on both quality *and* price, so contracting authorities have to justify why they appreciate a certain quality feature, and why they allow it to compensate a higher price. This is much more explanation and justification than is usual in automatic lowest-bid awards.

Another tempting but sometimes misleading thought about lowest-bid awards is that they force tenderers into a price competition while the quality can be ensured at the level that we have fixed. While theoretically this is correct, we should also be realistic about what a possible price war can mean on the actual sustainability of quality as promised at the tendering stage. Since in lowest-bid awards the price is the only award criterion, firms have no incentive to supply any quality that goes beyond pure technical compliance. While in one-off supplies this may be absolutely justified, this should make us think twice in the case of, say, long-term services contracts, for example buildings maintenance. In order to win such a contract in a lowest-bid award to begin with, firms have to compete on the price alone, so they are incentivized to cut their prices, in theory until the price equals their marginal cost, meaning that a profit margin of even one cent will be enough. If the contract is strategically important to them, they may even accept having no profit margin at all. Lowest-bid awards do not necessarily have this effect all the time, of course, since pricing depends on many factors other than marginal costs. Firms may ask higher prices if they have enough work already, for example; they may not find it worth it below a certain profit margin, or they have publically known and non-negotiable fixed rates; consultancies that make it their business to tender for each and every call have a certain price, and they will sometimes lose and sometimes win; universities can be of high quality but still win against consultancies on the price in a call for a research contract simply because PhD researchers tend to cost less than consultants do. We simply recommend keeping in mind the risk that, if prices are calculated too sharply, and margins are too thin, a firm that has succeeded in becoming the contractor will have little margin of manoeuvre on its quality either. If costs rise, or unexpected costs appear in the course of contract performance, or if there had been a miscalculation in the price offer that had narrow margins to begin with, the contractor may start losing money and decide to cut quality in order to compensate for this: use fewer staff, allocate less time, replace experienced employees with junior or temporary staff, etc. True, quality standards may be laid down in the contract, but contractual penalties or judicial remedies are not always the most helpful way to enforce quality where the contractor simply cannot afford keeping such standards at the contractually agreed prices.

Lowest-bid awards are simple and well-suited in cases where technical parameters are so clear that the only difference between admissible tenders is their price. As an anti-abuse tool, however, the usefulness of this award method is limited, and other safeguards are necessary. If anything, price-quality awards are in principle better at preventing abuse, because the award of quality points requires more justification than does an award on price alone.[15] In contracts where quality must be sustained over a longer period, it is in any case not a good idea to make firms compete on price alone at the tendering stage. Price-quality awards take some of the price pressure off tenderers, and allow them to calculate prices in a more quality-oriented and sustainable way.

---

[15] See also Chapter 13 on anti-abuse measures.

CHAPTER 6
THE PRICE SCHEDULE

Whether we award a contract on the basis of the price or cost alone, or on the basis of the price-quality ratio, in each case we will have to establish what a tenderer's price actually is. Prices are often expressed in model price schedules, which are templates that tenderers must fill in to give their total price and, where applicable, a breakdown of their total price by item. Typically, then, the price indicated in the bottom line of the price schedule is used to compare different price offers. The main challenge in designing price schedules is to express accurately what exactly is needed. A fair price comparison is only possible if all tenders compete to offer a solution to the same problem.

6.1. TOTAL PRICE

The easiest cases, as regards the design of price schedules, are those where a specific single product has a specific total all-inclusive price: a car, say, or an oven including delivery and installation. Let firms write their price into the price schedule, and, if you award to the lowest bidder, take the cheapest tender that is technically compliant. If you award to the best price-quality ratio, take the fixed price from the price schedule and relate it to the quality. In case more than one unit is needed, for example 80 fire extinguishers and 15 fire hoses, let the tenderers fill in their unit prices for each item, and let them multiply them by the necessary number of units. The bottom line will reveal the total price on which tenders will be compared.

Figure 6. Model price schedule with multiple units

Item	Unit price	Quantity	Price offer
Fire extinguisher	€70	80	*€5,600*
Fire hose	€350	15	*€5,250*
Total price			*€10,850*

6.2. CONSUMPTION MODELS

There are cases where it is not possible to specify in advance how many units exactly will be needed. In framework contracts, for example, it is almost by definition impossible to guarantee a precise consumption. We may need to replace one heat pump out of three if it breaks down, and we may need to purchase 3,000 metres of cable, but just as likely 4,000 metres. This is why framework contracts typically contain only unit prices, and, ideally, an estimate of the number of units that will be ordered. But even direct contracts sometimes need quantitative estimates: the installation of a relatively large piece of equipment that requires works in a building might also require a number of hours of unforeseen extra work. In such cases we simply have to try to establish our best estimate as a model of consumption over the contract duration in order to weight unit prices and compare total prices. If probably one out of three different pumps will need replacing, but not all three of them, the unit price of each pump should be multiplied by 0.33. For an estimated need of 3,500 metres of cable, the unit price per metre should be multiplied by 3,500. For an estimated 12 hours of unforeseen work, we may request an hourly rate multiplied by 12. Again, these are not necessarily the quantities that will actually be ordered, merely the quantities included in the price schedule to give tenderers an idea of probable quantities and to calculate realistic total prices, which will be then used to compare tenders.

What we should in any case *not* do is simply add raw unit prices, like one pump each plus one metre of cable. Otherwise, apart from the fact that the sum will have little to do with actually estimated spending, a company with inside knowledge could easily manipulate its price while honest outsiders needlessly inflate theirs, largely out of proportion to actual consumption. Here is an example with a mischievous insider (A) and an outsider giving honest prices (B):

Figure 7. Price comparison with unit prices, not weighted for probability of consumption

Item	Quantity	Tender A ("insider")	Tender B ("outsider")
Heat pump, Type 1	1	€10,000	€15,000
Heat pump, Type 2	1	€15,000	€20,000
Heat pump, Type 3	1	€20,000	€25,000
Cables (in metres)	1	€10	€5
Total price		€45,010	€60,005

Company A gave a low price for each of the heat pumps, because it knew that we will never order three pumps, while its competitor B needlessly inflated its total price. Conversely, A asked a higher price per metre of cable, knowing that many thousands of metres will be ordered. If however we weight the same prices for actually estimated consumption, it is clear that B, the honest outsider in this case, would win the award. In the price schedule below, both tenderers submit the same gross prices as above, but these prices are now multiplied by a factor that reflects probable quantities.

Figure 8. Price comparison with unit prices weighted for probability of consumption

Item	Quantity	Tender A ("insider")	Tender B ("outsider")
Heat pump, Type 1	0.33	€3,300	€4,950
Heat pump, Type 2	0.33	€4,950	€6,600
Heat pump, Type 3	0.33	€6,600	€8,250
Cables (in metres)	3,500	€35,000	€17,500
Total price		€49,850	€37,300

B's average pump is still more expensive than A's, but we will buy only one, not three, plus lots and lots of cables. Even if we buy the most expensive pump, the Type 3, together with our 3,500 metres of cables, B's price of €25,750 will still be better than A's price of €41,600.

6.3. THE VALUE OF AWARDS WITH CONSUMPTION MODELS

Apart from the fact that weighting unit prices for probability of consumption is fairer, it is also more transparent from a budgetary point of view: it is helpful if the total price in the price schedule also represents actual anticipated expenditure. In the first example above, when quantities were not weighted, the award for the pumps alone had a value of €45,000 assuming that A would have won the contract. In reality, the average amount of money to be spent on pumps, assuming that merely one out of three will need replacing, is just under €15,000. Meanwhile, B's honest price offer of €60,000 for the pumps alone might strike us as even more excessive, considering that presumably we had spent much less on pumps in all the previous years. But of course, with a price schedule that simply added raw unit prices, B's price offer was bound to have nothing to do with the actual amount of money to be spent. Apart from the risk of manipulation, there is just no need to inflate price schedules, and the published value of our award decisions, with quantities and prices that are unrealistic.

6.4. THE IMPORTANCE OF ACCURATE ESTIMATES

When we weight unit prices for probability of purchase, our estimates must be as realistic as possible. If, for instance in the case of unforeseen extra work hours, our estimate is too high, and we actually order just 6 instead of 12 hours, we may realise that, had we estimated 6 in the beginning, another firm would have won the award and the overall works would have been cheaper. Conversely, if our estimate is too low, for instance in the case of cables, a firm that already knows us can give a lower unit price using economies of scale, knowing that real consumption will be much higher than what is indicated. This is simply unfair at best, and an illegal distortion of competition at worst. Estimates remain estimates, of course, but there are means to improve them. Unexpected works are more probable in the case of an old building, where we find all sorts of pipes and cables behind the walls that no-one knew of, and less probable in a modern storage hangar. If the consumption really is uncertain, at least we should be transparent about it, and state clearly in the tender specifications what the amplitude was in previous years and what the factors are that might influence real consumption upwards or downwards: number of visitors, changes in legislation, the duration and results of test runs, the weather. This allows firms to make better informed price offers.

6.5. ADJUSTING TO DIFFERENT PRICING POLICIES

There are specific economic sectors where price comparison is not straightforward simply because the pricing models differ between firms. Firms offering car-related services might charge their clients per car, or per year, or per kilometre, or per transaction. Thus, when designing a model price schedule, it would be unwise to let tenderers enter their annual fee if some of them do not actually charge per year in the first place, and have other fees instead. Knowing all relevant fees is however crucial to calculate cost and compare tenders. One contracting authority may have few cars but lots of mileage, whereas another has lots of cars but low use per car per year. Different pricing models will have a different impact on total cost. One way to solve this would be to let tenderers themselves list their fees in whatever format they find appropriate, and compare cost on the basis of a reference year, with so-and-so many cars and so-and-so many kilometres, as determined in advance. This does not mean that this will be exactly the volume of consumption, but it is a tool to compare costs in a realistic way – whether we award the contract based on price, cost, or price-quality ratio.

6.6. INCLUDING COST IN THE PRICE

As noted earlier, there are cases where it is sensible and legitimate to consider lifecycle cost as part of the price to be paid for a product, namely where costs can be quantified in money terms, and where they differ between products so that firms can compete on cutting these costs. Thus, the true price of a car may include the price we will have to pay to dispose of it later, and the fuel costs we will have to bear while using it. This is after all expenditure that we will have to accept one way or another; making it effectively part of the purchase price allows us to minimize these costs because cars with a lower disposal cost, a longer warranty and lower fuel consumption will show up as being cheaper, which is in fact true of course. Other indirect costs related to the purchase of a car are more generally the costs of ownership, meaning costs that we have to pay simply for owning rather than leasing a car: this includes taking care of tyres, insurance, technical inspections and resale.

A somewhat problematic indirect cost item is the cost of changing from one supplier to another, known as switching costs. In purely economic terms, it is absolutely true that if a new contractor company will require us to make investments in order to adapt our IT infrastructure, for example, then these costs are part of its price. The problematic aspect is that factoring in switching costs will favour the incumbent, whereas much of public procurement law is precisely designed to *break* the bias for existing contractors, and open the field to competitors. Still, public procurement law should also be concerned with economic efficiency – hence the focus on free and fair market competition – and if switching costs are a reality, then ignoring them is inefficient. Presumably procurers will find other ways to favour their current contractor; but rather than make them write selection criteria that no-one can meet except their current contractor, we prefer to let them express their cost perception in honest and objective terms. In this case, it would be via switching costs. However, if a challenger company actually manages to be competitive even including these switching costs, then there is no longer a reason to deny it the contract.

The above solutions apply to cases where infrastructure migration to accommodate a new contractor is not part of the old contract. In fact, the more efficient solution is of course to include decommitment costs as part of the original award, allowing us to make the incumbent take care of the removal of infrastructure for a new awardee. In general, contracts should not expose the contracting authority to a buyer lock-in: authorities should not have to stick with the incumbent contractor in a monopolistic situation for years simply because maintenance must be carried out by the manufacturer, or because the contractor continues to own intellectual property right to, say, IT infrastructure. Where these lock-ins cannot be avoided, switching costs should still not come as a surprise when awarding a follow-up contract.

In addition to indirect costs, the 2014 EU Public Procurement Directive also explicitly authorizes the calculation of external costs such as environmental pollution and CO_2 emissions.[1] External costs, also known as social costs, are costs that are not borne by the one who caused them but by society at large, and environmental pollution is a classic example. Internalizing external costs by making them part of the overall price can follow a policy objective in public procurement, in that it makes market participants feel that things like pollution are not actually for free. Firms that succeed at reducing their carbon footprint will have an advantage because, all else equal, their final price will show up as being lower than the one of their less green competitors.

In practice, if we can monetize costs, meaning reliably expressing them in currency units based on a method that is the same for all tenderers, and if these costs are likely to differ between tenderers, then we should by all means include them as an element in the price as cost. This can be done by either letting firms indicate lifecycle or other indirect costs in the price schedule, or by adding such costs ourselves. In case we cannot monetize these costs, because their amount depends to some extent on subjective appreciation – for example the dangers of having to handle toxic materials, hazardous emissions other than CO_2 – then the alternative is to award the contract based on the best price-quality ratio and include these costs as a quality criterion. The lower the indirect or external costs, which would then be expressed in a better quality score, the better the overall quality; the better the overall quality becomes, the more we accept a higher purchase price; and the better the quality becomes at stable purchase prices, the better the ratio.

6.7. PRICE INDEXATION

For long-term contracts, it is a common practice to provide for an indexation of the price in order to take into account inflation, meaning changes in overall price levels. Otherwise, if costs rise but the prices in the contract stay the same, a company may end up losing money over the years. As a result, it may not tender in the first place or, if it does, ask a higher price from the start in order to compensate in advance for the expected rise in costs. In markets with low competition but volatile producer costs, the absence of indexation can lead companies to collude with each other, and coordinate prices between each other to rig the game, rather than expose themselves to the risk of real competitive bidding under conditions of uncertainty regarding future costs.

---

[1]   Article 68 (1) (b) of Directive 2014/24/EU.

6.7.1. THE LOGIC OF INDEXATION

Indexation as such means that the prices which are fixed in the contract are linked to the development of a specific price index. An index is a figure, published regularly by a statistical office or other government agency, a sectoral syndicate or a financial consulting agency, which expresses overall price levels based on either a single price or, more pertinently, on the aggregate of a number of individual prices. The most common form of indexation – though not always the most sensible one – is to link contractual prices to consumer price inflation. In that case, the development of the general consumer price index for the relevant geographical area determines the adjustment of the price in the contract. If inflation was at 2% over one year, prices in the contract are increased by 2% as well.

An index can be either based on a baseline or it can be chain-linked. In a baseline index, price levels in a certain year are fixed as 100, and price levels in all subsequent years are calculated in relation to that year. In a chain-linked index, by contrast, price developments for each year are expressed in relation to price levels the year before. In both cases, however, the application of indexation to the contract price is the same, because the only thing that matters for this purpose is the percentage increase, or decrease, between the current index and the previous index. The formula would in any case look like this:

Old price × (current price index / previous price index) = New price
For example:
€500 × (129 / 126) = €512

In the example, the current index is about 1.02 times the previous index, meaning that prices rose by slightly over 2% since the last index.

In the case of a monthly index, if price adjustments are annual, the first reference index and all subsequent indices could be those for the second month before the month of the signature of the contract and each anniversary, as it stands on a certain day, for example the last day of the month preceding the month of each anniversary. For a contract signed in December, for instance, the relevant index would be that of October as it stands on 30 November each year. The purpose of the time period allowed ahead of the price adjustment is to make sure that the index is already published when the calculation is to take place. The purpose of fixing a certain day is to take into account that some indices are revised after their first publication, and that they are sometimes recalculated to refer to a new baseline or reference year. For example, it may be that October's index is slightly corrected in January, or that the price level in the year 2020 becomes the new 100, as a chain reference or baseline index for the following decade. This will have no consequence for our contract, since year-on-year comparisons between indices will remain possible as before. Thus, choosing an index *as it stands on a certain day* is simply a measure of legal certainty.

6.7.2. AUTOMATIC AND MANUAL PRICE ADJUSTMENT

The price adjustment itself can be automatic, meaning that prices are adjusted every year and it is not necessary to make any special request. This means, if prices tend to rise, that the contracting authority has to remember raising prices if the contractor forgets it, or pay the accumulated difference later, when both remember. Alternatively, the adjustment can be carried out upon specific request by one of the parties. Typically, again assuming that overall prices rise rather than fall, it is the contractor who will routinely request a price adjustment upwards. All this is a quasi-automated form of price adjustments which is part of normal contract performance. Otherwise prices would have to be renegotiated and changed through a contract amendment; this, however, is problematic and possibly illegal in the case of public procurement because it would basically mean a new award with bigger payments but without competition.[2] Price adjustment under indexation is not a new award, however, since it forms part of the conditions of the initial award and had been known to all tenderers from the start. Besides, indexation gives greater certainty to the tenderer that prices in fact *will* be adjusted: a normal contract amendment can be refused by the contracting authority, while normal price adjustment under indexation cannot.

6.7.3. UPWARD AND DOWNWARD ADJUSTMENT

In markets where price levels tend to fluctuate, it may be in the interest of the contracting authority to provide for a downward adjustment as well. After all, there is no need, in principle, to keep paying old prices when real costs to the contractor are down, because then we are basically just paying to fatten the company's profit margin for no reason. However, the mere possibility of downward adjustment can also mean that firms will increase their initial prices to begin with, to compensate in advance for any future price reduction, or that they will not tender at all. Often, therefore, indexation clauses provide that prices can be adjusted upwards but not downwards, or that they can also be adjusted downwards but never below the initial price that applied at the signature of the contract.

---

[2]   See the case C-454/06 *Pressetext* and the very detailed Article 72 of Directive 2014/24/EU on contract modifications.

6.7.4. TO INDEX OR NOT TO INDEX

When drawing up the tender documents and the model contract, we have to answer two principal questions. The first is whether we want to index prices at all. For short-term contracts it normally does not make much sense, and even for two-year contracts, in sectors where generally prices are stable, it may not be worth the administrative effort. It does make sense to index prices if otherwise tenderers would increase their initial prices more than it would cost us to manage the indexation, or if otherwise competition would be significantly reduced because most potential tenderers will simply not make any offer at all, or if the eventual contractor refuses to prolong the contract in order to get out of the old price obligations. Considering what all *that* would cost us, it is surely justified to invest a little effort once a year to recalculate prices and to document the adjustment. Cost-sensitive contracts in volatile markets may even require indexation at an ever higher rhythm, as no company would otherwise agree to sign any contract.

6.7.5. THE CHOICE OF AN APPROPRIATE INDEX

The second question we have to ask ourselves, if we do index prices, is what the relevant index should be. As noted, the most basic index is consumer price inflation in the country of performance. In case of cross-border contracts within the European Union, we might choose inflation in the contractor's country, inflation in the country of performance, or the harmonized consumer price index for the EU or the Eurozone as a whole, which is published by Eurostat, the EU statistical office, and which is widely used for contract indexation.

However inflation, in the sense of the development of consumer prices, is calculated statistically on the basis of a basket of products that the average consumer buys, including food, clothing and consumer electronics. Inflation for the general consumer does not necessarily mean that producer costs are also rising in the economic sector of our contract. If we buy office paper, for example, general inflation says very little about the production costs of paper. Here the costs of raw materials are much more important. On construction sites, the market price of concrete is, for some firms, the single most decisive cost factor. An indexation of works prices to general inflation will not be helpful at all if the price of concrete suddenly doubles. Meanwhile, the cost of labour-intensive contracts, like consultancy services, software development or low-tech maintenance, will be mostly determined by labour costs – salaries and other employment-related expenses – but labour costs do not always rise in line with inflation either. The changing cost of road transport services is mostly the changing price of fuel. In all of these cases, if we index our prices to consumer price inflation, we risk that our contractors will either keep increasing their prices without any justification, or the opposite, namely that the indexation does not cover the rise in actual costs.

To choose a suitable index, we need to know at least roughly the cost structure in the sector we are addressing, in other words the reality in which companies operate. For that we recommend consulting with either industry associations or companies themselves, as part of market research before the call for tenders, or directly as part of a competitive dialogue with companies in the course of designing the tender specifications. If it turns out that the main cost factor is labour costs, or a specific raw material, then this will help us choose an index, a formula and a revision rhythm to match this reality. If the main cost factor is the amortization of machines – an expensive machine is bought at the start of a contract and its value decreases over time, showing up as losses in the accounts – then there is no need for indexation at all. That is because amortization is not an actual loss, but a mere bookkeeping operation to spread out investment costs over several years and, by treating them as losses, save taxes. Regarding labour costs, if salaries are increased nationwide by an administrative decision, or by a new collective labour agreement, then this can even be translated into contract prices immediately, without waiting for the next contract anniversary.

Regarding the practical application of indices, we recommend simply seeking the advice of the statistical offices that publish them. These can be either national agencies or, in the case of the European Union, Eurostat, which publishes on its website a whole range of official price indices free of charge, including the HICP harmonized consumer price index and, for labour-intensive contracts, the labour cost index (LCI). Labour and other producer cost indices are also published at national level, often with a granularity sufficient to cover a particular sector, such as construction or transport services. Private consultancies offer paid access to indices as well, for example on the aggregate world market prices of certain commodities like metals.

Another alternative to fixed indexation, at least for dynamic sectors, is to provide, from the start, for a mid-term review of the contract, in order to check against overall price level benchmarks and insert a price update where necessary. This is less automatic than a classical indexation, but it is not an entirely arbitrary price hike either: in fact, in sectors with rapid technological innovation, prices could well be adjusted downwards as both hardware and software becomes cheaper to produce and more widely available. To ensure certainty at the tendering stage, the basic conditions for this mid-term review should be fixed at the outset, certainly if prices are raised rather than lowered with respect to the initial tenders. As for indexation to general inflation, meaning consumer prices, this still remains an option and can be safely used for generic contracts that have a long duration, low cost volatility and not a very high value. This ensures that there is in any case *some* price adjustment, which is more or less right on average, and which at least encourages tenderers to bid. For high-value awards with very specific cost factors, however, an unsuitable price indexation can be very costly, and it should therefore make sense to make inquiries and perhaps hire a business consultancy firm for a one-off advice. There will be a small fee to pay for that, of course, but the potential savings – in the form of more competition and more efficient pricing – will certainly outweigh them.

CHAPTER 7
QUALITATIVE AWARD CRITERIA

In price-quality awards, when we award a contract not on price alone but on price in combination with added quality, we have to define and evaluate that added quality. And it is up to us to define what kind of quality we are looking for. Article 67 (2) of the 2014 EU Public Procurement Directive gives a list of examples of possible quality characteristics, but in fact there is an infinite number of quality criteria: robustness, softness, colour, choice, eco-friendliness, speed, flexibility, ease of use, to name but a few possible quality features. It all depends on what *we* appreciate. And by "appreciate" we mean "accept paying extra for". Let us not make the mistake of believing that price is price and quality is quality. The two are linked, because the more points a firm collects for its quality, the more expensive it can afford to be. Thus, each additional quality unit has a monetary value, which can even be calculated in advance. The higher a tender's proposed quality is, the more it will justify a higher price. Which is, of course, exactly what we want, because if only the price mattered to us, we would choose a lowest-bid award.

7.1. THE CHOICE OF AWARD CRITERIA

So what kinds of award criteria are allowed? As far as EU procurement law and case-law is concerned, contracting authorities enjoy a very wide margin of discretion in choosing, and checking against, qualitative award criteria, meaning criteria other than the price.[1] The main requirement is, of course, that we publish in advance what we are looking for, so that tenderers will know when drafting their offers what award criteria are important to us. Evidently we cannot change or fix our award criteria after the submission deadline or after the opening.[2] Furthermore, we must not mix up selection and award criteria:[3] selection is to check firms' capacity, while award is based on the quality of their

---

[1] See cases C-31/87 *Beentjes*, C-513/99 *Concordia Bus Finland*, C-19/00 *SIAC Constructions*.
[2] See cases C-31/87 *Beentjes*, C-87/94 *Commission v. Belgium*, C-470/99 *Universale-Bau*, C-331/04 *ATI*, C-532/06 *Lianakis*, C-19/00 *SIAC Constructions*, C-448/01 *EVN*, T-461/08 *Evropaiki Dynamiki v. EIB*.
[3] See cases 31/87 *Beentjes*, T-387/08 *Evropaiki Dynamiki v. Commission*, C-315/01 *GAT*.

tenders. Nor should we draft award criteria so as to favour a certain company, notably our current contractor.[4] And whenever we appreciate quality, we must consider *verifiable* quality. It is potentially unlawful,[5] but also simply unwise, to award a contract to a firm, and reject other firms, based purely on what that firm has promised us, without there being a means to check whether it is actually true.

In addition to classical or immediately economic quality features, we may wish to reward other aspects of a product in order to promote a broader policy goal. The hiring by the contractor of long-term unemployed persons, or the environmental sustainability of products,[6] are, at least under EU law, perfectly legitimate qualitative award criteria as well. The same holds true for the share of employees with long-term rather than short-term contracts, or the share of employees from socially disadvantaged groups – in a firm as a whole or, if this would be unrealistic in a certain sector, in certain functions within the firm.

Judges – at least the European Court of Justice when it comes to EU procurement law – do not tend to involve themselves too deeply in the choice of desired quality aspects or the evaluation of the content of tenders, because this is the primary responsibility of the contracting authorities. Instead, judges will readily check whether procedural rules and the duty to state reasons have been respected, whether the facts are correctly appraised, whether there has been a manifest error of judgment or an abuse of power.[7] The larger the margin of discretion, as is the case in procurement, the more important it is to be diligent and impartial, to observe procedure, and to explain reasons.[8] But judges are unlikely to say that there have not been enough points for a certain award criterion, or that another award criterion should have been added.

The question in practice is therefore not so much whether a certain award criterion is allowed or not – because almost everything is allowed – but whether that award criterion corresponds to an actual need. The basic rule, to which we will keep coming back, is the following: If we think that a certain quality is absolutely necessary, then we should make it a minimum technical requirement for all tenders; if we have defined what quality we need, and are not willing to pay anything extra if there is more of it, then we should not make it an award criterion; if we have defined what quality we need, but *are* willing to pay extra if there is more of it, *then* we are talking of an actual award criterion.

---

4   See cases T-148/04 *TQ3 Travel Solutions*, C-234/03 *Contse*.
5   Case C-448/01 *EVN*.
6   See also Chapter 12 below on green procurement.
7   See cases 56/77 *Agence Européenne d'Interims*, T-169/00 *Esedra*, par. 95, T-148/04 *TQ3 Travel Solutions*, par 47.
8   See cases C-269/90 *Technische Universität München*, T-44/90 *La Cinq*, par. 86.

7.2. QUALITY VERIFICATION

We cannot identify quality without evaluation, and it is unwise to award contracts based merely on what companies promise us. In fact, under EU law it may be downright illegal.[9] These are unverified quality claims, and awards on that basis are known as cheap talk awards.

Let us make no mistake: firms competing for a public contract know the rules of the game. It is in the firms' interest to maximise their fulfilment of award criteria as defined by the contracting authority. In a positive sense, this is both obvious and welcome. After all, the conditions of the call for tenders are there precisely to incentivize companies to offer what the buyer wants to obtain. If it is clear from the call that the price decides, firms have a strong incentive to offer their cheapest acceptable product and thus indeed to compete on the price. If many points are reserved for environmental criteria, firms have an interest to offer environmentally friendly solutions, since this is apparently what the evaluators will reward: the more points firms obtain for environmental quality at constant prices, the better their price-quality ratio and the higher their chances of winning the contract will be. The danger emerges when award criteria are difficult to verify, and firms use this to design their tenders in an almost manipulative way. They then essentially tell the contracting authority what it wants to hear, while making an aggressive price offer that normally could not support the high quality that is promised. For example, if an award criterion states that the winning company should invest in continued environmental quality management once it has the contract, it may be easy for firms to offer a low price, promise whatever is necessary to win the contract, and then still execute it in the cheapest possible fashion to maximize profits.

To address the risk of cheap talk deciding the award, there are several things we can and should do. We completely agree that promises made at the tendering stage should be fixed as a legally binding engagement in the final contract.[10] This is typically done by annexing the original tender as an integral part of the contract. But while this gives the contracting authority a legal enforcement tool, we should not forget that a freshly awarded contract typically means a certain lock-in situation for the authority itself. Conducting a new call for tenders to find a new contractor costs time and effort, so authorities may be reluctant to terminate a contract that they already have, or even to impose penalties on their

---

9   See case C-448/01 *EVN*. In that case, an electricity supply contract had been awarded taking into account the electricity's renewable sources; in fact, it turned out that the contracting authority had no means to actually check whether the electricity bought came from renewable sources or not.

10   S. Onderstal & F. Felsö, 'Procurement Design: Lessons from Economic Theory and Illustrations from the Dutch Procurement of Welfare-to-Work Projects', in K. Thai, ed., *International Handbook of Public Procurement*, Boca Raton: CRC Press 2009.

contractor – even when a private client would have imposed penalties or terminated cooperation with the bad contractor long ago.

Therefore verification of actual quality should ideally take place already at the award stage. This is easier in the case of supplies, where for example a certain machine with certain quality features is offered. If it turns out that the awardee can only deliver a cheaper and simpler model, and not the one that was promised, we can deny acceptance, withhold payment, renounce the contract and re-award it to the second-placed tenderer. We might even consider imposing an administrative sanction for giving false information, if we realize that it had been clear from the outset that the content of the winning tender could not be delivered. Quality verification is more complex in the case of works, as well as services, however, where the possible insufficiency of the quality delivered will become clear only later. There the risk has to be managed mainly though continued monitoring, quality checks along the way, and deferred final reception where the last payment is either reserved, or covered by a bank guarantee, until the result is satisfactory. At the tendering stage, the quality of the performance of a construction company or service provider would mainly have to be assessed indirectly. We can assess the quality of the tenderer's proposed work planning and methodology, and make it an award criterion with a minimum threshold, such as a minimum of 10 quality points out of 20. So if already the planning is amateurish or unfeasible or otherwise inappropriate, we can reject the firm on quality grounds. Furthermore, selection criteria help us limit the competition to companies that are experienced, so there is a hopefully lower risk of bad performance. In addition, we can, even though this is an extreme case, determine that the price offered is abnormally low, and reject the firm for that reason.[11] The qualification of prices as abnormally low can be a tool to fight against bid-rigging, price dumping,[12] and other types of manipulation, but it might as well be used to say that the price is unrealistic so the performance of the contract is bound to be bad.

What if we lack the capacity – the technical means or the expertise – to evaluate the quality of tenders, or the quality differences between them? Of course there are clear cases where evaluation can only be plausibly carried out by the users themselves. Thus, we do not need any external technical experts to tell us whether a website is easy to use, or whether the offered furniture is aesthetically appealing or not. Only we can tell. It becomes more complicated when, for instance, in the case of furniture, one of our award criteria is "robustness". This we can either evaluate in a low-tech way, by requesting

---

[11] Under EU law, firms must be given an opportunity to respond to the allegation that their price is abnormally low, and to possibly explain why their price is so competitive. Still, the contracting authority must make the final judgment. See Article 69 of Directive 2014/24/EU and cases C-76/81 *Transporoute*, T-4/01 *Renco*, T-148/04 *TQ3 Travel Solutions*, T-121/08 *PC-Ware*, C-599/10 *SAG ELV Slovensko*.

[12] See case T-121/08 *PC-Ware*.

samples and basically sitting on them, and jumping up and down on them, to see whether they can take it. But if the contract is to cover a great number of units over several years, or if the equipment will be unusually strained, it might make sense – unless we know ourselves how to do it – to have their robustness tested by an expert bureau. The bureau will then apply industrial standards on how much weight from which direction a piece of furniture must be able to tolerate. Naturally they will charge us a fee, but in relation to the value of the overall contract, and the risk that comes with insufficient quality, this fee may well be worth paying.

In general, if we are unable to verify quality differences between different products, then we simply should not make them award criteria. Award criteria are, after all, those features on which a tender can distinguish itself from the others, which it can only do if the distinction is in fact recognized by the evaluators. If we cannot recognize the differences, then instead we can either prescribe the quality as a technical minimum for all tenders and evaluate only those things that we actually can evaluate, or prescribe an overall minimum standard and award the contract to the lowest bidder. Alternatively, if we still want to encourage competition on a quality aspect, but cannot judge which product is better, then outside help in the form of external experts can be hired. Any of these solutions is better than inviting quality competition on things that will look all the same to us. For the result will be that everyone gets more or less the same quality score, so that only the price will decide: we end up buying the cheapest product, not the one with the best value for money.

What we said earlier concerning selection criteria largely applies to award criteria as well, in that the order of the steps in the thinking process should start at the beginning, not the end. Under selection criteria, the first question is not what kinds of proofs we want companies to send us, but what kinds of risks we foresee for the contract performance stage. Selection criteria follow from risks, proofs follow from selection criteria. In the case of award criteria, the first question is not how to verify a certain quality aspect either. The first question is what quality means to us, which aspects we want all tenders to have, and which aspects we would be ready to pay extra for. The latter become qualitative award criteria, for which we need to find a means of verification, with outside help if necessary. If it turns out that our desired criterion is actually unverifiable, we should reconsider our approach.

7.3. COST AS A QUALITY CRITERION

Is lifecycle cost an award criterion, or simply part of the price? Article 53 of the old EU Public Procurement Directive 2004/18/EC explicitly suggested that operational costs are a possible quality criterion, whereas for a contracting authority cost is also a broader expression of what it will have to pay on top of the purchase price. The new Directive 2014/24/EU, in its Article 67, no longer mentions cost as a quality criterion, but it does not exclude it either. We suggest a golden rule. If costs can be reliably expressed in currency units, as is the case in lifecycle costing, then they should be part of the price. If costs can be merely approximated, and are thus at least partly a matter of subjective assessment, then they should receive a quality score and count as a quality feature, with an appropriate weight, along with the other qualitative award criteria.

CHAPTER 8

THE PRICE-QUALITY RATIO

Awarding public contracts based on who has the best price-quality ratio is certainly the smartest award method, and intelligent drafting of award criteria is an art form of its own. As noted earlier, if we announce that we will award our contract to the firm with the best price-quality ratio, we are basically making known that we accept paying a basic price for basic quality, but that there are quality features for which we are prepared to pay extra, and that to us the cheapest is not necessarily the best. In this chapter we will discuss how to carry out such an award in practice: how to calculate the best price-quality ratio by dividing a tender's quality by its price, how to weight the price criterion and the quality criterion and adapt the formula accordingly, and how to evaluate the quality in such a way that the outcome reflects our true perception.

8.1. PRICE-QUALITY RATIOS AND OTHER FORMULAS

While private buyers can afford to appreciate a product's quality and its price tag in an implicit, intuitive, holistic and mathematically fuzzy way, public buyers need to make explicit their choices. They normally do that by expressing their quality perception in a numerical score, and by relating that score, through a formula, to the price offer. In a price-quality award, the winner is not necessarily the tender with the lowest price, nor necessarily the one with the highest quality, but the one who offers the most advantageous price-quality ratio. The easiest and most immediate way to see a tender's price-quality ratio is to literally divide, for each tender, its quality by its price. This shows us directly and objectively how much quality is offered per euro. The winner is the firm which, for every additional euro we spend, gives us the most extra quality in return.[1]

We must point out that the formulas which are most broadly used in practice today do not actually produce any price-quality ratio, and have other

---

[1]   The formula that we developed, with its adjustment to the weight of award criteria, will be published in Ph. Kiiver & J. Kodym, 'Price-Quality Ratios in Value-for-Money Awards', *Journal of Public Procurement* (2015), forthcoming.

shortcomings as well.[2] One widely used method, for example, is to first convert prices into points, and then to add the result to the quality score. The problem with this method is that, first, the conversion of prices into points is needlessly complicated. Some of the existing formulas are so hyper-mathematical that probably neither the firms nor the procurement officers themselves can predict what score will be generated for any given price. The second problem of the conversion of prices into points is that, even when the formulas are relatively simple, they are often discriminatory. This is the case whenever the difference between price scores is not proportional to the differences between actual prices.[3] In other words, the curve on which price offers find themselves is not linear, so tenderers in different price ranges are arbitrarily disadvantaged. The third problem is that, even when the formula is simple and results are linear, the conversion of prices into points is still typically not based on the expectations of the buyer but on the prices that are offered. For example, often the lowest price automatically gets the maximum score, no matter how high that price actually is. In other words the best price benchmark is not fixed by the buyer, but by the tenderers themselves, because what is measured is not the amount of money that tenderers ask but merely the price differences between them. The fourth and related problem is that, when we in the end add a price score to a quality score, the overall result is not a ratio but a sum. This allows even poor-quality tenderers with high prices to collect points on both quality and price, even though their value-for-money may be unacceptable. Certainly when a market is carved up between just a few dominant firms, they can afford to offer barely acceptable quality at exaggerated prices, and still collect points for both. Since the formula *adds* quality and price, instead of *dividing* quality by price, the result does not show how much – or how little – quality per euro is offered. The fifth problem of adding quality scores and price scores, instead of generating a ratio between the two, is that, depending on how the weighting of criteria is translated into the formula, the price criterion can be inadvertently neutralized if its weight is below 50%. If there are 30 price points and 70 quality points to be collected, any firm that is 31 quality points below the next tenderer is out of the game, even though its tender is technically compliant with the tender specifications, simply because even with the best price score that firm could not possibly compensate the difference. It is absolutely possible that, in certain contracts, the quality criterion weighs more heavily than the price does; but then this should mean that it is easier for good quality to distinguish itself from basic quality, not that it becomes

---

[2]   J.L. Fuentes-Bargues & C. González-Gaya, 'Analysis of the scoring formula of economic criteria in public works procurement', *International Journal of Economic Behavior and Organization* (2013), pp. 1–12. See also F. Waara & J. Bröchner, 'Price and Nonprice Criteria for Contractor Selection', *Journal of Construction Engineering and Management* (2006), pp. 797–804; N. Dimitri, 'Best Value for Money in Procurement', *Journal of Public Procurement* (2013), pp. 149–175.

[3]   See Appendix II for practical examples.

impossible to compete in lower price ranges, certainly if this had not been announced in the call for tenders itself.

It is for all these reasons that we recommend, instead, to simply divide each tender's quality in points by its own price in euros. Since we do not convert the price into points but use the price itself, we avoid the weaknesses of price scoring; and since we generate a ratio for each tender independently from the content of the other tenders, we are not only able to easily compare competitors with each other, but also to make sure that any given tender offers enough quality per euro, irrespective of the price range as long as tenders are technically acceptable. In the past some procurers may have shied away from the quality-divided-by-price method, arguing that it only works if we have a single quality criterion and if the weighting between quality and price is 50:50. In fact, we will show that it equally works in case of multiple quality criteria, and that we have developed a very simple method to adjust the formula to any weighting we want. But first things first.

8.2. QUALITY DIVIDED BY PRICE

The basic principle to calculate a tender's value for money is to divide, quite literally, value by money. In other words, the quality score gets divided by a tender's price offer.

$$\frac{\textbf{Quality}}{\textbf{Price}}$$

The result is the amount of quality in score units for each currency unit. If the currency is euros, then the contracting authority will see exactly how much quality it will get for each euro that it is going to spend. Let us say we want to buy office furniture, and we received four tenders, A, B, C and D, offering different quality at different prices.

Figure 9. Price-quality ratios under the Q/P formula

Tender	Quality score	Price	Quality/Price
A	50	€10	5.0
B	66	€12	5.5
C	60	€15	4.0
D	75	€15	5.0

A is the cheapest and offers 5 quality per euro. B is more expensive, but its higher price is more than compensated by its higher quality. It means that, compared with A, its price increased but its quality grew faster. C is even more expensive, but here the high price is not justified: it offers less quality per euro than the first two tenders. D offers the same value for money in a high price range as A does in a low price range. They are tied: in order to win, D would have had to offer an even higher quality than it just did, or a slightly lower price than it just did. The final outcome is that B wins. Not because it is the cheapest (it is not), nor because it offers the most expensive luxury (it does not), but because it offers the most quality per euro. C loses so badly not because it is so expensive, but because it hardly offers any additional quality for each additional euro that it charges.

8.3. ADJUSTING FOR CRITERIA WEIGHTING

The only practical adjustment that needs to be made to the formula concerns the weight of the price and the quality criterion. The weight of the price criterion indicates how important it is to us that offers be cheap; the weight of the quality criterion indicates how much more we are willing to pay extra to obtain a better quality, rather than basic acceptable quality. A weighting of 90:10 in favour of the price signals to firms that 90% of our award decision will be determined by the price, so we will accept a minimal extra charge for better quality and, above all, their offers should not be too expensive; the less the price weight, the more we want firms to compete on both price and quality.

8.3.1. THE BASELINE QUALITY SCORE

The weight adjustment to the formula is simple: we take the weight of the *price* criterion, and we give that number as a baseline *quality* score to all tenders. Thus, if our weighting is 75 (price) : 25 (quality), then we give all admissible tenders 75 quality points from the start. Basic quality will stay at 75, the best can get up to 100; in the end, everyone will have their final quality score, which will be somewhere between 75 and 100, divided by their own price.

Now why is that? Why do all offers start out with a baseline quality score, such as 75, and not at zero? It is because already our basic acceptable quality represents a certain quality in absolute terms, and because even that basic acceptable quality comes at a certain price. If three-quarters of maximum desirable quality is already mandatory for everyone, as it is in our example, then real quality competition starts at 75 points and unfolds over the remaining quality margin of 25 points. The quality margin corresponds to the price margin, in that three-quarters of maximum acceptable spending are reserved to buy basic quality, and the remaining quarter can be spent on quality that goes beyond minimum requirements.

As in every price-quality award, and irrespective of which formula we are using, we as buyers must start out by defining what the minimum acceptable quality for us is, and what market price corresponds to that minimum quality. Second, we must define on which additional quality features tenders should try to distinguish themselves, and thus for which type of additional quality we are willing to pay extra. Third, we must determine what the maximum price is that we are willing to pay in order to obtain the maximum quality that is useful to us.

For example, let us say that a basic acceptable mobile phone, with a battery standby time of 10 days, costs €60, but we are willing to pay up to €80 for a phone that has a standby time of 20 days. Our quality criterion is therefore "standby time". Since the price corresponding to basic quality in proportion to the maximum acceptable price for the highest quality, in other words 60 divided by 80, is 0.75, it means that 75% of the maximum price we will pay just to reach minimum acceptable quality. The remaining 25% of the price we are willing to spend to obtain better quality. Our price-quality weighting, as we publish it in our call for tenders, is 75:25 in favour of the price.[4] This also means that 75% of the maximum number of quality points are used up just to reach minimum acceptable quality. This is why everyone starts at 75 points out of 100. Real quality competition will take place over the last 25 points.

Figure 10. Baseline quality scores corresponding to the price weight under the Q/P formula

Minimum acceptable quality (€60) 75 quality points	Extra quality (€30) 25 quality points	Total quality scores
Tender A: 10 days of standby		75 + 0 = 75
Tender B: 15 days of standby		75 + 12.5 = 87.5
Tender C: 20 days of standby		75 + 25 = 100

In the above example, tender A proposes a phone that merely complies with minimum requirements, and thus receives no extra points on top of its baseline score, since it does not add any supplementary quality that would justify a higher price. B offers half the maximum supplementary quality, meaning five out of ten extra days of standby, and therefore receives, on top of its baseline score, half of the 25 extra points that we can award, in other words another 12.5 points,

---

4   Strictly speaking it is not a weighting, in the sense as it is used when two scores of different weight are added together, since we are not actually adding but dividing. It is however the functional equivalent of weighting, it is understood by tenderers as such, and it can therefore safely be published as such. Procurers who are using a formula other than Q/P are advised to double-check the way they establish their weighting: whatever they do, basic quality at basic price must in any case in the end obtain the same final score as best quality at maximum acceptable price. For the remainder of this book we continue with the weighting as it is described in this chapter, and as it is used for adjusting the Q/P formula.

assuming that we add quality points in a strictly linear fashion. C not only complies with minimum requirements but also satisfies our maximum need, and thus gets the baseline score plus the full additional points. In the end, the quality scores are 75, 87.5 and 100, respectively, and they correspond to the overall quality of each product, namely a common value for compliance with basic specifications plus the individual added value in line with quality criteria. Each tender's quality score then gets divided by its own price to determine who has the best price-quality ratio.

Our quality estimates will obviously not guarantee that actual tender quality will be as neat as this. It may well be that we are willing to pay up to a certain amount for maximum useful quality, but that none of the tenderers actually proposes such a quality. In that case no-one will reach the maximum quality score, which is not a problem since they can still achieve a good price-quality ratio.[5] It could also be that a tenderer offers insufficient quality, for example less than 10 days of standby time, in which case the tender gets rejected as technically non-compliant, irrespective of its price-quality ratio. And it could be that a tenderer offers excessive quality, meaning more quality than we are willing to pay extra for, for example 30 days. In that case the offer's quality reaches, and stays at, the maximum score, because 20 days represented maximum usefulness to us already, and the 21st day is not worth any more money to us.

Still, assume, for the purposes of our example, that tenderers A, C and B presented basic quality, maximum useful quality, and quality half-way between the two, respectively. After quality evaluation, the division of the quality score by the price determines the ratio between the two, which in turn decides who the winner is.

Figure 11. Price-quality ratios under the Q/P formula at 75:25 price-quality weighting

Tenders	Basic quality score	Added quality	Total quality	Price	Quality/Price
A	75	+ 0	75	€50	1.50
B	75	+ 12.5	87.5	€90	0.97
C	75	+ 25	100	€100	1.00

We may notice that the price offers we received in the example do not exactly correspond to our estimates: the basic phone is cheaper than expected, and the best is more expensive than we were willing to pay. Indeed, just like quality estimates do not guarantee any particular tender quality, initial price estimates are never a guarantee that these will be the prices we are going to pay: in fact it may be that even the cheapest offer we receive costs more than our maximum

---

5   We should not make the mistake of automatically giving the maximum score to the best quality among the offers received, because in that case evaluation expresses not quality in relation to our needs, but just quality in relation to other tenderers.

acceptable price, either because we misjudged market prices, or because we were unlucky with our tenderers. Still, the initial estimates allow us to fix a price-quality weighting in order to tell firms what kind of extra cost proportion we are willing to accept to go from basic to best. And this helps us keep costs under control.

In the above example, the basic offer A has the better price-quality ratio and wins. And of course it does: after all B is hardly better but costs almost twice as much, C is a merely a third better and costs exactly twice as much. Our weighting was 75:25 in favour of the price, which means that, whatever the price range of tenders actually submitted, the best product can cost only up to a third more than the basic solution and stay competitive. Here the cheaper offer A wins the award quite comfortably. We might also turn it around: A costs about half as much as B, but provides almost the same quality.

The beauty of this method – quality divided by price and quality evaluation starting at a score corresponding to the price weight – lies, among other things, in the relative proportions of the total quality score. First, a weighting published with this formula in mind sends a clear message to the market operators about what we are looking for. If a firm reads our tender specifications, and imagines the corresponding basic product from its own catalogue or from its competitors' catalogue, it can immediately position itself within the market and propose a solution offering best value for money for the contracting authority. If its best product is only a quarter more expensive than the basic solution, it surely makes sense to offer it to us, and we may profit from a higher quality at a moderate price increase. This calculation on the part of tenderers is much less straightforward under other formulas, where the price score entirely depends on the bids received, and where tenderers are therefore largely forced to guess.

Second, the proportions of the award criteria remind us that even a basic solution – deserving zero additional points for extra quality – has a certain price. If the weighting is 75:25, it means that the basic product is at 75% of the whole, let us say "perfect" product, and that we can expect to spend three-quarters of the money to obtain just that basic version. This may seem obvious, but it is far from clear in some traditional methods.

Third, starting the evaluation at a baseline quality score, as we propose, compensates for a certain psychological drawback that manifests itself in real life. When communicating evaluation results to unsuccessful tenderers, it is frustrating to have to tell a company which had proposed a good-quality solution that it received only 10 out of 25 points. The tenderer will be forgiven for feeling offended, for the score does convey a message of poor quality or mediocrity, which in this case is neither fair nor correct. It is just that most of the quality the tenderer proposed had been obligatory anyway and therefore does not show up in the quality score anymore. Incidentally, it is also understandable if evaluators feel uncomfortable giving a mere 10 quality points to a good-quality tender, which might in fact lead them to inflate scores, thereby compressing quality differences for everyone.[6] However, if we can write, instead, that the score was 75 plus 10, meaning 85 out of 100 in total, the message is already much more positive. The result is still the same – the tenderer was unsuccessful – but the score reflects much more fairly and much more correctly the tender's actual overall quality content: the tender was at 85% of maximum quality. Perhaps there was someone else who offered more quality for the same price, or slightly less quality at a significantly lower price, but either way there was nothing wrong with the quality itself.

8.3.2. THE PROPORTION OF EXTRA SPENDING

Theoretically, if our weighting is 75:25 and the basic phone costs €50 as above, a maximum-quality phone could afford to cost €66 and beat the basic phone with an even better price-quality ratio; at €67 it already costs too much. Wait a minute: had we not just said that we would pay up to €90 for the best phone? Yes, we said that, but then we were assuming that the basic phone would cost €60. Now that the basic phone is actually cheaper, there is no reason to pay a greater multiple of that basic price than is necessary. As noted, thanks to our 75:25 weighting, we made sure that, whatever the price for the basic model is, the best one can only be a third more expensive.

What if we appreciated a longer standby time much more than we just did? What if we were willing to pay three times as much for a maximum standby time, meaning to go from €60 up to €180? In that case quality would matter twice as much as the price, our price-quality weighting would be 33:67, everyone would start at 33 quality points from the start, and compete for the remaining 67 on quality before having their score divided by their price.

Figure 12. Price-quality ratios under the Q/P formula at 33:67 price-quality weighting

Tenders	Basic quality score	Added quality	Total quality	Price	Quality/Price
A	33	+ 0	33	€50	0.66
B	33	+ 33.5	66.5	€90	0.74
C	33	+ 67	100	€100	1.00

Now that we find quality much more important than the price, tender C with the maximum-quality phone has no difficulty winning the award. The fact that it costs twice as much as the basic phone does not disturb us, considering that actually we would even have been willing to pay thrice as much. Thinking about

---

6   See Chapter 9.4 below on what we call point inflation.

our preferences allowed us to fix a weighting, which tells firms what we expect them to do, in this case not to be shy and to propose us a very good phone.

Of course, phones do not become more or less expensive just because we are willing to spend more or less on extras. Market prices are market prices. However, the important point is precisely that the monetary value of an added quality trait in our own perception is not the mere difference between two price tags: it is the expression, in currency, of how much it is worth *to us*. Economists speak of utility, in other words usefulness. In a functioning market, prices are already a fairly accurate expression of the utility of products to most consumers. But it may be that a feature that is cheap in money terms is actually highly valuable to us (having a mobile phone with a camera in it, for example, which we appreciate a lot even when cameras come almost for free). Or it may be that a feature that is expensive in money terms is simply not interesting to us, so we would pay hardly anything for it if it were offered (a high-end camera with even more megapixels, say, even though we already have plenty of megapixels in a normal phone). In both cases we should weight the quality feature based on our theoretical acceptable extra cost, not necessarily based on the real market price. In the first case, we thereby strongly encourage firms to include the feature, even if it is much cheaper than what we would have been willing to spend on it theoretically; in the second case, we may be pleasantly surprised if an offer includes the feature at an unexpectedly low price, in other words a price which is lower than what we thought was the usual market price. In both cases, having made the features an award criterion, we can reward to a higher or lesser degree added quality, without having to exclude companies that are not able to provide these features at all.

8.3.3. ADJUSTING THE SCALES

Regarding the minimum quality score in case of price-quality award, we use a range of 100 simply for the sake of convenience. Thus, if the weighting is 80:20, then all tenders offering at least basic quality should get 80 points out of 100, but they might as well get 160 out of 200, or 8 out of 10, or 4 out of 5. What matters is not the number but the proportion.

What if we divide quality by price and find that price-quality ratios are inconvenient because there are too many zeroes in the decimals? Say an excavator has a quality of 78 points, and costs €112,000. Its ratio is 0.000696. No problem: just divide all tenders' prices by 100,000, and get rid of the first five zeroes. Our excavator will show a price-quality ratio of 69.6, which is already much nicer. It is not strictly necessary, but in high prices ranges it is generally easier to calculate in kiloeuros or megaeuros. The relative proportions stay the same – as long as the same is applied to everybody's prices, of course.

8.4. MULTIPLE AWARD CRITERIA

So far we considered examples where we had the price criterion and one quality criterion, such as "longer standby time" in a mobile phone, much like "faster response time" in services, "longer warranty" in works, or "less noise" in a dishwasher. But the same logic is followed when we define more than one qualitative award criterion. We simply add up all the extras we are willing to pay for, and for each criterion its share of the total price determines its weight.

For example, let us say that we want to buy printer cartridges, and the basic acceptable supply deal should cost us €60,000. However, on top of that we would appreciate an after-sales service, desktop delivery rather than delivery to a central depot, and the knowledge that the cartridges are made from recycled materials. Now that we know what we are willing to pay extra for, all we need to do is determine how much each extra quality aspect is worth to us.

Figure 13. Price-quality weighting with multiple quality criteria

Basic quality requirement	Basic price	Share of the total price at maximum quality (€95,000)
Printer cartridges	€60,000	0.63
Quality criterion	Maximum acceptable price	Share of the total price at maximum quality (€95,000)
After-sales service	€10,000	0.11
Desktop delivery	€20,000	0.21
Recycled materials	€5,000	0.05
Total price at maximum quality	**€95,000**	

The above calculation means that our overall weighting is 63 (price) : 37 (quality). The quality here is the sum of the weights of all individual quality aspects. If we assess total quality on a scale of 0 to 100, then all offers will start at 63 points.

Figure 14. Quality assessment with multiple quality criteria

Basic compliance	After-sales service	Desktop delivery	Recycled materials	Total score at maximum quality
63 points	+ 11 points	+ 21 points	+ 5 points	100 points

An offer that includes only cartridges and no service, only central delivery, and no recycled materials, will obtain and keep 63 points, and have that divided by its price. A tender that offers the basic package and adds desktop delivery will obtain 63 + 21 = 84 points in total, and have these 84 points divided by its price. It is also possible to round off slightly to facilitate evaluation, such as, in this case, 65 – 10 – 20 – 5. An offer that fulfils all our extra wishes to the maximum will either way obtain full supplementary points and have 100 in total, to be also divided by its own price.

The inclusion of the recycling criterion in our example is, by the way, a reminder that not only purely economic criteria but also social and environmental considerations can be expressed in the price-quality weighting. Such criteria are explicitly allowed under EU procurement law,[7] but even they need to have some objective value. It is not enough to say that we appreciate green materials. If we make it an award criterion, then it means that firms that fulfil it can allow themselves to be more expensive. And it is up to us to determine how much extra cost we are willing to tolerate. At least for our internal calculations – without necessarily putting any exact figures into the contract notice – we must decide how much it is worth to us. If it is actually worth nothing, then it should not be an award criterion; if we find it so important that all tenderers must have it, then it should not be an award criterion either, but a minimum requirement for everyone. If we accept tenders without it but appreciate if they have it – meaning that we accept paying more for it – only then can it be a genuine award criterion. The social or environmental criterion will then simply become part of overall quality, along with the other, more traditional criteria.

8.5. MULTIPLE OBJECTS

In cases where we purchase an entire list of objects, each item to be evaluated separately, the price-quality ratio can also take into account the heterogeneity of the items. Think of, for example, office supplies, which include staplers, perforators and envelopes. Unless we are able to give a global quality score for the catalogue of products as a whole, it is necessary to arrive at an aggregate quality score for the catalogue that results from the evaluation of the individual items.

If all items have the same weight, meaning that they are all equally important to us and that they all represent equal shares of total spending under the contract, then the sum of all quality scores can simply be divided by the tender's total price. If some products are more important to us than others from a quality point of view, we can weight items by multiplying quality scores with an importance coefficient. For example, if we find it twice as important to have high-quality envelopes as to have high-quality staplers, we can multiply the quality score for the envelopes by a factor of two. This increases the quality weight in relation to the price.

---

7   Cases C-31/87 *Beentjes*, C-513/99 *Concordia Bus Finland*, see also Article 67 (2) (a) of Directive 2014/24/EU. See also Chapter 7 on the choice of award criteria above and Chapter 12 on green procurement below.

If different items have a different financial weight, we will have to weight (again) quality scores for this fact as well. Think of a case where we will be spending two-thirds of our money on one particular product on the list, and the rest on the remaining fifty products. Weighting quality in proportion to financial importance can be done either in advance, by fixing a specific weight for a specific product that will be the same for all tenders, or afterwards, by using products' share of the total price for each tender individually. The first option, with fixed weights, is useful in case there are relatively few items on the list. Thus, we estimate the relative value of staplers and envelopes, determine that we will be spending, say, 80% of our money on envelopes, and weight the quality score of envelopes and the other products accordingly.

Figure 15. Weighting of item quality with fixed weights

Item	Gross quality score	Quality importance coefficient	Quality score weighted for quality importance	Fixed weighting for relative volume	Net quality score
Envelopes	60	× 4	240	0.8	192
Staplers	70	× 1	70	0.2	14
Total quality score of the tender					206
Total tender price (in thousands of euros)					3.1
Q / P					66.45

In the above example we find the quality of envelopes four times as important as the quality of staplers, which is why we expanded the quality spread for this product by the factor four. In addition, since we established that we will be spending 80% of the money on envelopes, we multiply the quality score for that item again, this time by 0.8. The same exercise is repeated for all other items and tenders, obviously using, for each tender, the same coefficients for the same items.

The second option of weighting for item shares of the tender price rather than for fixed weights, meanwhile, is useful in case there is a very great number of items. In that case, each unit price is multiplied by the probable number of needed units, the result being the total cost of the item in question, and this result is multiplied by the respective item's quality score. The financial weights of each item can therefore slightly differ between tenders. In the example below, the net price of envelopes as proposed by the tender represents 81%, rather than 80%, of that tender's total price, and the item's quality is weighted accordingly.

Figure 16. Weighting of item quality depending on the pricing of the tender

Item	Gross quality score	Weighting for volume				Quality importance coefficient	Net quality score
		Unit price	Estimated quantity	Total price	Weighted quality score		
Envelopes	60	× 0.05	× 50,000	/ 3,100	48.39	× 4	193.56
Staplers	70	× 3.00	× 200	/ 3,100	13.55	× 1	13.55
Total quality score of the tender							207.11
Total tender price (in thousands of euros)							3.10
Q / P							66.81

We repeat that this second method of tender-based weighting should be used only if there are many, say several hundreds of items in the price schedule, and that otherwise the method should be one of fixed weights for all tenders. The reason is as follows. If the weights depend on the relative price of items within the tender itself, the result is that the more expensive a particular item is in comparison with the rest, the heavier this item will weigh in the final scoring. Tenderers might increase the price of a good product in order to make it weigh more heavily, while the impact of this price increase on the total price can be minimal; conversely, if a company offers a high-quality item and makes an effort to lower the price, it is penalized because the more it brings the price down, the less the item will weigh. When there are few items, the effect can become unfair, and we therefore recommend fixed weights for all. When there are hundreds of items, this effect becomes negligible, however: weight differences will be smaller, and tenderers are perhaps more likely to simply offer all items from a catalogue in a certain quality range, rather than to start fine-tuning item by item. Thus, for longs lists of items, the weighting can more readily be done based on tender prices themselves. Tender-based weighting after all does not rely on initial estimates, which can be inaccurate, but on actually offered item prices, and it is therefore more closely in line with actual spending.

8.6. GLOBAL QUALITY AND MINIMUM QUALITY THRESHOLDS

It should be noted that the earlier examples tended to describe an award based on one basic product plus extra features, like cartridges plus desktop delivery, or mobile phones plus longer standby time. But it works exactly the same for cases where it is overall quality that is assessed. Take for instance the commissioning of a research study: we do not normally say that a study must meet a number of minimum requirements and then offer extra features. In the end the study as a whole – grasp, methods, feasibility – must be good. Still we can very well estimate a price range between basic and best, and that is all we need to fix our price-quality weighting. A basic study, carried out by a single graduate student, may theoretically comply with minimum requirements, whereas a study by a team of professional researchers from a good university will easily cost ten times as much. If we are willing to pay ten times more to go from basic to best, then our weighting is 10:90. All tenders start at 10 quality points, and will have all of 90 points to compete for, in what is a heavily quality-oriented call for tenders.

To tackle the danger of receiving poor-quality offers, meaning offers that are formally compliant with tender specifications and have a good price-quality ratio but a poor quality in absolute terms, we have the option of imposing minimum quality thresholds. In that case, even where a tender formally corresponds to our requirements but is not good enough, it gets rejected if its quality score is below a cut-off point. In the case of the research study, for instance, it is absolutely possible and legitimate to announce that, of the maximum 90 quality points that can be awarded, a tenderer must obtain at least 50 points, meaning 60 points out of 100 in total, or at least 60% of points for each sub-criterion.

From a theoretical point of view this poses something of a puzzle, because now we seem to have *two* thresholds of minimum acceptability: the very low one, on formal compliance, and a higher one, reflecting minimum desired quality. The reason is that in this particular case we are unable to define a basic "model" of a product, in the way we do with phones or dishwashers. The distribution of the first 50 points between formal compliance (10 points) and the minimum quality threshold (60 points) is so fuzzy that we cannot plausibly express them in explicit criteria. Tenders must simply make enough sense. Only once a tender has attained 60 points on quality does real competition on price-quality ratios start.

This is exceptional and will occur mostly in intellectual services contracts, much less in supplies or works. Yet in our research study, since formal compliance is simple but minimum acceptable quality is hard to define, each criterion indeed does have two weights. For *internal* purposes, if our quality threshold is 10 + 50 = 60 points out of 100, then it means that our weighting is really 60:40 in favour of price. A study by a team of junior researchers which we find acceptable in quality terms can therefore compete against a high-quality study by a senior team costing 1.5 times as much. For purposes of conveying a realistic message when *advertising* the call, however, we should still publish the much more quality-heavy 10:90 weighting. This is to stimulate quality competition, and to avoid the impression that price matters more to us than it actually does. Nevertheless, in the details of the call we should clearly explain that a cut-off threshold will be used and where it lies.

Figure 17. Formal compliance at one-third and minimum quality threshold at two-thirds of maximum quality

Formal compliance	Rejection for insufficient quality	Competition on price-quality ratios
Real price weight for internal purposes = 67		Real quality weight = 33
Published price weight = 33	Published quality weight = 67	

In the example shown in the table above, 33 points are awarded to formally compliant tenders, meaning for instance tenders that propose a research study that correctly identifies the purpose of the study. Tenders awarded less than 67 points in total are nevertheless rejected, without having their price-quality ratio calculated. Only tenders scoring at least 67 points will compete for the remaining 33 points on quality and have their price-quality ratio determined. Real competition between qualitatively acceptable tenders will unfold under a 67:33 weighting, but summary advertising may well announce the inverse 33:67 weighting while stressing that a quality threshold will apply. In all other, less exceptional cases, there is no need for a separate quality threshold, because the basic acceptable compliance already serves as a single and decisive cut-off point that determines the sole applicable weighting of award criteria.

8.7. THE DILEMMA OF HIGH QUALITY STANDARDS

Let us assume that we want to buy a new reception desk for our entry hall, and that only the best is good enough: we want this to be a prestigious, presentable, high-quality piece of furniture. Does this now mean that the weight of our price criterion is very low, since we will not shy away from added expense to get what we want? Or does it mean the opposite: since our minimum requirements are already so very high, there is not much more of a quality difference a tenderer can possibly make?

The answer lies in the way we have formulated our technical specifications. If we said that we need a reception desk, full stop, then the basic model might indeed be very simple and we can pile up award criteria to incentivize firms to add more and more quality, almost irrespective of the price. However, if we describe already as a basic requirement that the desk must be custom-made using certain exquisite materials, then indeed it may be that 90% of what we want is already mandatory, so the weighting will be 90:10 in favour of the price. And indeed, it may be that we have already described *everything* we want, so the award can actually just go to the lowest bidder.

Criteria weighting is not an indicator of absolute quality standards or absolute prices in euros. It merely denotes what we are willing to pay extra in proportion to the basic price. That basic price, in turn, corresponds to our minimum acceptable quality, which can be either very basic indeed, but which can be already quite high from the beginning. Starting at a basic minimum quality means rejecting bad offers for having a poor price-quality ratio, because high-end solutions will easily generate a better price-quality ratio even when they are more expensive; starting high means rejecting poor offers as technically non-compliant, for only the best quality on the market will have its ratio calculated to begin with.

And yet again, we must stress what we had already mentioned earlier, namely that if we truly want to unleash competition on who supplies the finest quality, a lowest-bid award is not the most efficient way to do that. After all, in lowest-bid awards, or in price-quality awards where the price is the overwhelmingly dominant criterion, firms are incentivized to cut their prices, and to not offer anything that goes beyond minimum requirements. If we want to incentivize firms to go beyond the minimum quality, a quality-heavy price-quality award would make more sense, all else being equal.

8.8. ON THE NEUTRALIZATION OF THE PRICE CRITERION

The 2013 Rules of Application of the Financial Regulation, which is the basic text regulating procurement law for EU institutions in their capacity as contracting authorities, prohibited contracting authorities to design their price-quality award in such way that the price criterion gets neutralized.[8] What does that mean? Different EU contracting authorities seem to have found different answers to that question. In our view, the purpose of the rule is to avoid cases where a public buyer looks at quality alone, takes the best, and pays the firm whatever it wants. Indeed, the 2014 Directive, which applies to the member states, features a much more nuanced clause: award criteria must not give unrestricted freedom of choice to contracting authorities.[9]

So is the price criterion already neutralized, and is choice already unlimited, if its weight drops below 50%? With a price-quality ratio method as we propose it in this book, we think not.[10] Even a weighting of 40:60 simply means that we are willing to pay two and a half times more to obtain the best quality, instead of basic acceptable quality. In other words better-quality offers will find it easier to

---

[8]   Article 149 (3) of Delegated Regulation 1268/2012.
[9]   Article 67 (4) of Directive 2014/24/EU; see also C-513/99 *Concordia Bus Finland*.
[10]   There are other formulas where a drop of the price weight below 50% actually does neutralize price differences, see Appendix II for examples. This does not happen in our formula, though.

justify a higher price, but the moment they cost more than 2.5 times the basic price, they will lose. The price criterion is by no means neutralized, and choice is by no means unlimited. Some authorities have fixed an internal rule, albeit using different formulas, saying that the price should have at least a weight of for example 20%, but this is an individual policy choice rather than a universal rule. Other methods are possible as well to encourage strong quality competition without neutralizing the price criterion.

For instance we might assess quality alone but fix a budget ceiling or a lump sum for each awardee. Research institutes, for example, can be told that the budget for each commissioned study is limited or fixed, and that as long as they stay below that limit or accept the lump sum, there is a free range of pure quality assessment. Effectively, there is no weighting against the price criterion anymore, meaning that quality becomes the only award criterion, and that the only difference between tenderers is therefore their quality, assuming that they all will ask or accept the same price.[11] The same holds true in regulated markets where prices are fixed for the whole sector. In that case there simply is no price competition, so again the only real competition, given identical prices, will be just about quality. But this does not mean that the price criterion is neutralized, in the sense of conferring an unlimited choice on the contracting authority, because the contracting authority will still have to justify its quality assessment under previously known quality criteria, and award the contract to the offer proposing the highest value *given that prices are constant*.

It should be added that, when the price-quality ratio of tenders is calculated in the way as it is described in this book – with quality assessment starting at a baseline score that corresponds to compliance with basic technical requirements – even a weighting of 0:100 in favour of quality will not neutralize the price criterion. It will simply mean that the basic acceptable solution has no intrinsic value at all, and that tenderers are free to compete over the whole quality range. Of course normally a basic acceptable solution *does* represent a certain quality in itself, and it *does* cost something, like a car without air conditioning, if the presence of air conditioning is an award criterion. But if the tender specifications are drafted in such way that formal compliance with the specifications is not yet worth anything in money terms, and all absolute quality comes from quality *increases*, the award will still not be arbitrary irrespective of prices. Instead, as always, the award will go to the tenderer who presents the best price-quality ratio, in this case with 20 quality at a certain price winning against 80 quality as long as 80 quality is more than four times as expensive.

The greatest practical danger of price neutralization in real life presumably emerges in cases where the contracting authority does not look at the prices themselves, but where it converts them into points, and does so in such way that

---

11   Article 67 (2) of Directive 2014/24/EU provides explicitly for the possibility of pure quality competition under a fixed price.

price differences are neutralized as an erratic and unintended result of the formula it uses. This price neutralization occurs when everyone ends up having more or less the same price score,[12] or where in certain quality ranges it becomes mathematically impossible to win the award irrespective of how competitive the price is.[13] Even the most expensive bidder can win on quality alone if his or her price gets converted into points and he or she obtains more or less the same number of points as the lowest bidder, or where the price criterion is neutralized because an implicit quality threshold exists below which tenderers cannot possibly win. For example, under a formula where the quality score is added to, instead of divided by, the price score, the weight of the price criterion must stay at least at 50%. If it is lower, it means that there can be a quality difference of a certain number of points between two tenders, while there are not enough price points available to compensate that difference, so not even the maximum price score for a very competitive price will ever tilt the balance. Quality thresholds are not problematic as such, but they are unfair if they are not published and instead result implicitly from the price conversion formula, and if firms and perhaps even procurers themselves are unaware of this effect. These are two of the several reasons why we do not want to start converting prices into points to begin with. Our formula uses the price as such, in currency units, not an artificial score; and if we divide the quality score by that price, as we do, then we obtain a price-quality ratio that allows us to award our contract to the firm that offers most value for money.

Yet another way of stressing quality in the evaluation, without changing, let alone neutralizing, the price weight, is to ask tenderers to submit their technical offer and their price offer in two different envelopes. Evaluators will then consider and rank the content first, and open the price bids afterwards, so that prices will not subliminally influence the evaluation. Even outright favouritism becomes harder, because in order to make sure that the preferred tender wins on a better price-quality ratio without knowing the prices of the other tenderers, it would be necessary to inflate drastically its quality score. And still, another tenderer with a decent quality score can surprise the evaluators with a very competitive price and thereby score a better ratio.

It is true that two-envelope evaluation can be burdensome and inefficient in cases where there are proofs missing regarding exclusion and selection criteria, and where these have to be compiled first before making a selection decision and starting to evaluate the content of tenders. However, in cases where exclusion and selection proofs are necessary only with respect to the presumed winner of the award,[14] the evaluation of tenders can start immediately on the

---

[12] J.L. Fuentes-Bargues & C. González-Gaya, 'Analysis of the scoring formula of economic criteria in public works procurement', *International Journal of Economic Behavior and Organization* (2013), pp. 1–12.

[13] See Appendix II for examples.

[14] See for example Article 57 (2) of Directive 2014/24/EU.

content – first on quality only, then on prices, and finally on the ratio between the two.

8.9. THE IMPORTANCE OF KNOWING WHAT YOU WANT

An honest and accurate expression of our weighting is important to both the buyer and the seller. If we make the price criterion too heavy, say, firms will believe that mostly the price decides, so they will not risk offering a high-quality product that costs more. When, as a consequence, all the tenders we get are simple and cheap products, we will realize that actually we would have been happy to pay a little extra for a better product, and we will regret having undervalued the quality criterion. The opposite is also disappointing: overvalue the quality criterion, making firms believe that quality counts and price is secondary, and all or most tenders will be relatively expensive. Again, correct weighting is important to both sides of the economic transaction of public procurement: it shows what we want, and it shows firms what we want them to offer.

In reality inaccurate weighting does probably not occur because we misjudged what is available on the market, but because the weighting is fixed based on a pre-existing standard template, without taking into account our actual preferences. Thus, a contracting authority may have issued an internal policy guideline for all affected procurers stating that, for certain types of contracts, a price-quality award with a certain weighting is recommended. And so we take 60:40 for a supplies contract, because this is recommended, and start thinking what on earth we should put as quality criteria. Once we are done, we let ourselves be surprised by the content of incoming tenders. Maybe the recommendation was absolutely appropriate, but it may also turn out that we end up paying too much for things we do not really care about. Say the quality criterion we came up with is an eco-label. If the weighting is 60:40, and price-quality ratios are calculated as fair and linear ratios as we describe them in this book, and if a supply deal without an eco-label costs €100,000, then a company *with* an eco-label can afford to charge us €166,000, all else equal, and still win the contract. Are we really willing to pay €66,000 extra on an eco-label?

Templates can make routine jobs easier, but public buying is rarely a routine job. If we really want an eco-label, we can make it compulsory for everyone and, if the rest of what we need is already defined, launch a lowest-bid award. If we do not care about eco-labels, we leave them out altogether. If we want to encourage tenderers to obtain and propose eco-labels, and are willing to accept that an eco-label contract might be €10,000 more expensive, then our true weighting is not 60:40 but around 90:10.

8.10. DEFINING QUALITY IN PUBLIC PROCUREMENT

Having considered the methodological foundations of relating price to quality in public procurement, let us come back to a very fundamental question: what is quality, how do we define it, and how do we express it in a call for tenders? Conceptually this is probably the most challenging question to answer in this context, and yet it has to be answered each and every time, for only then does the application of a mathematical formula on price and quality reflect the buyer's preferences.

Quality as such can refer to a firm's internal quality assurance as well as to the quality of deliverables, meaning the quality of the actual product.[15] Quality assurance, often referred to as quality management, covers an organization's systems, processes and procedures set up to avoid mistakes and failures in delivering quality products and services to customers. It is often documented and certified, for example under the ISO 9000 series or other international and national certification standards. Quality management systems are meant to provide a certain level of assurance to clients that the contract will be performed in an organized and streamlined manner, because the firm's internal processes are organized and streamlined to begin with. In public procurement, it is therefore primarily the object of selection criteria, rather than award criteria: tenderers may be required to have their quality management documented and certified, under a specifically named or any equivalent certification standard, if this requirement is linked to a particular quality risk, especially in manufacturing, building or complex work contracts.[16] The presence of a quality assurance system on its own however does not say much about the quality of the deliverables. The quality of the products or services that we actually wish to receive needs to be defined in the technical specifications, and it may be defined even further under qualitative award criteria, if tenderers are to be incentivized to add quality that goes beyond minimum requirements.

In order to reflect on, and design, specifications and award criteria with a view to describing the desired quality, we suggest the following practical steps:

1. *Evaluate* the existing contract and past calls for tenders. Are we, and are the current contractors satisfied with the current contractual arrangement, with the current performance, and with the process in which the contract had been awarded? Lessons from previous calls can and should feed into future calls, for example in the form of reworded specifications, different award

---

[15]   ISO, *International Standard ISO 9000: Quality Management Systems – Fundamentals and Vocabulary*, Geneva: ISO Copyright Office 2005, p. 1.

[16]   See also Article 62 of Directive 2014/24/EU.

criteria or in fact a different award method altogether, different contract clauses, or stricter or more permissive selection criteria.[17]

2. *Research* the market and learn what the available solutions are and how much they cost. As companies specialize and innovate, developing new solutions and ancillary services, contracts can improve from a quality perspective as well. In the past companies and administrations were buying, maintaining and selling their service cars, for instance; today's fleets tend to be fully managed by operational leasing companies while their customers focus on their core business. More flat-rate solutions, which are easier to manage on both sides, and innovative financing facilities appear. We as public buyers cannot follow this pace in all domains, but we need to be informed – having talked to potential suppliers, for example – about possibilities before launching specific calls in order not to circumscribe too narrowly a potentially outdated solution. Where we are key accounts, meaning big clients, we may even enjoy the benefits of an unusually customized solution, in which case an award procedure with negotiation would be useful.

3. *Brainstorm* on what quality means to us in the future contract, in an exercise involving managers and users. What would we appreciate having, what is an absolute must, what would make our life easier? At this stage, we should be ends-oriented as much as possible, and think in terms of deliverables and not specifications, describing in a human language what we understand by quality. Any easy and straightforward technique can be employed, like attaching Post-its onto a flipchart, one for each aspect. One Post-it could be reserved, as a joker, to stand for good and bad surprises, defined in a broad but understandable way, such as ease of management or simplicity of use. Just think of normal private buying: we may realize that a newly purchased hi-fi audio set does not have any buttons on it, and can be operated only via the remote control. This can be a plus for aesthetics-minded customers, but a huge minus for customers who tend to lose the remote, or who expect that the remote will break more easily than the set itself. Public buyers will have to be able to express real but unexpected quality difference somehow.

4. *Translate* the collected ideas into specifications and award criteria. The field of identified quality aspects should essentially be divided into two segments. One segment should be reserved for those aspects that are mandatory, meaning that tenders that lack them will be rejected by definition: these are the technical specifications with their minimum requirements. The other segment should be reserved for quality aspects that are not strictly necessary but whose presence would add value, for example in administrative cost savings, comfort, prestige, efficiency, promotion of social and environmental goals, customer or citizen satisfaction, etc., and on which tenders can further distinguish themselves. These are award criteria. If Post-its have been

---

17   See also Chapter 11.2 below.

attached to a flip chart, they would now move either to the left or to the right. If all features end up as being mandatory, it means that desired quality is exhaustively defined and the only remaining award criterion on which tenders can compete is the price.

5. *Assign price tags* to those quality aspects that remain in the segment for award criteria, if there are any. These price tags represent the amount of money we would be willing to pay in order to obtain these features, or to obtain them at the highest desired quality. These prices correspond to the utility we derive from the quality in question, meaning its usefulness to us; they will usually be close to real market prices, which ideally represent utility to consumers already, but they do not necessarily have to be close to market prices. Our price tag can be below the market price if we find a feature mildly useful, but refuse to buy it for what it normally costs: in that case tenderers are incentivized to include the feature only if they manage to offer it at a surprisingly low price. Conversely, our price tag can be above the market price if it is worth to us more than what it normally costs: in that case tenderers are incentivized to include the feature whenever they can, without worrying too much about the impact this will have on the total price.

6. *Calculate* the weighting of award criteria. The price tag corresponding to the minimum package under the technical specifications is the price corresponding to basic acceptable quality. Adding to that the price tags for the award criteria will generate the estimated price at maximum useful quality. Dividing the basic price by that maximum price will generate the publishable weight of the price criterion, while dividing the single price tag or each individual price tag for the award criteria by the maximum price will generate the publishable weight of each of the qualitative award criteria.

7. *Verify* the quality as it is offered, and as it is delivered. Quality verification at the evaluation stage is crucial in order to base the award decision on actual quality perception; quality verification at the performance stage after the award is necessary to enforce contractual compliance, but also to make sure that what is delivered corresponds to the quality that had been promised in the tender, meaning that the award decision was justified. If award criteria are by definition not verifiable, or if we lack the means to verify them, or if after verification contractors can supply quality that deviates from what had been compared to other tenders at the award stage, the result is that competition is distorted, rendering the contract award more or less arbitrary. To stay with the example of Post-its, qualitative award criteria that cannot be verified or enforced must be removed from the flipchart at the very beginning.

CHAPTER 9
QUALITY ASSESSMENT

In price-quality awards, having established how much quality means to us in relation to the price, how can we fairly and sensibly distribute points to reflect our perception of a tender's extra quality? On a scale of 0 to 10, how many points should we give to a good offer, or a decent but not ideal one? Of course this will, and really should, depend on the subjective quality perception of the contracting authority. After all it is the contracting authority that is in the best position to determine what it wants, and to tell whether what it sees is what it wants. Office furniture can be good because it is beautiful, or because it is robust, or because it is produced in an eco-friendly manner. We would like to encourage contracting authorities, and their very much human procurement officers and evaluators, to express sincerely what they appreciate and how much they appreciate it. Qualitative award criteria are simply features that the contracting authority finds desirable, even if it costs more than the basic model does.

And yet, while we are largely free to choose what type of feature we appreciate and are willing to pay extra for, we normally will, at the end of the day, have to express our quality perception in terms of numbers: a quality score. We suggest distinguishing three types of criteria depending on their quantifiability. Let us call them (1) binary criteria, (2) quantitative criteria, and (3) non-binary qualitative criteria.

9.1. BINARY CRITERIA

Binary criteria are quality features that are either there or not. If we are willing to pay extra for a car with cruise control, and reserve 10 points for that, then the car with cruise control will get those 10 points and the car without it will get none. The same goes for phones with or without a camera, furniture with or without an eco-label, or machines that use more or less than 50 litres of water per hour. Already we see that the binary character of quality often lies in the way we draft our award criteria, because actually it is very well possible to appreciate better and worse cameras, easy and tough eco-labels, and more or less water consumption. Still, it may not always be possible, or worth the effort, to make such a distinction. In the end, a binary quality criterion is basically a lump sum of quality points that is relatively easy to award in a yes-or-no fashion. Supply delivery within two days? Yes. Delivery on Sundays? No. These are all perfectly legitimate binary criteria.

9.2. QUANTITATIVE CRITERIA

Quantitative quality criteria are those that are expressed as numbers to begin with, such as volts, seconds, or decibels, so all we have to do is put them in proportion to the maximum quality score. For example, we may require a minimum number of days of battery standby time in a phone, and be willing to pay extra for longer times. If the minimum acceptable time is 5 days, the ideal time is 15 days, and a firm offers us 12 days, then this means that this firm offers us 70% of the 10 supplementary days that we are willing to pay for. As a result, if our quality score function is linear, it should receive 70% of the extra points we had reserved for this criterion. Similarly, we may be willing to pay extra for machinery that comes with a ten-year warranty. If a firm offers us five years, it would, in a linear function, get half the points for that criterion. Or we might be willing to spend more on an office table if it can be quickly disassembled. So we order a sample, and clock the time it takes us to disassemble it. If we think that the process should be doable in 30 minutes, then 30 minutes get zero extra points, and models that are faster to disassemble get more points, up to the maximum score for what is the fastest time that we are willing to pay for.

The main challenge is to distribute tender scores correctly between the basic and the best. We should know what the minimum requirement corresponding to zero extra points is, and what the maximum desired quality is that merits the maximum score, so all offers will find themselves between the two in a way that corresponds to the relative usefulness of added quality from the buyer's point of view. Sometimes we may be tempted to fix a minimum but then say: the more the better. This will however not work very well, and is not actually realistic either. If the basic quality gets a basic score and the scoring is open-ended, under a rule of three, then a tenderer might theoretically get more points than are available. We might then try and cap this, by giving the maximum score to the best tender among those that we received, and distribute everyone else in between. But that is not a very good idea either, because it can mean that most points go to the least bad offer. Tenders will obtain points as a function of the content of other tenders, instead of as a function of their actual utility to the buyer. Imagine receiving three offers, each proposing products that are made of the cheapest plastic, where we would be willing to pay extra on stainless steel. None of them should receive maximum points.

Instead, a proper distribution of quality scores, by way of linear intrapolation or otherwise, requires not only a minimum level of acceptability, but also a maximum where we say that enough is enough. There must be a point where we say that this is sufficiently good, and from now on we will not pay anything extra. Economists speak of diminishing marginal utility, meaning that every additional quality unit is worth less and less to us, until we do not care anymore about further additions. That is precisely the point where we have to fix our maximum. For example, we may pay extra for a 10-year warranty, but whether it is 10 or 11 years makes no real difference anymore; disassembly of the table in five minutes is already perfect, and so we refuse to pay extra to go from five to four minutes.

The scoring does not always have to be linear. We can very well devise a quality scoring formula that increases sharply the number of quality points when going from two to three years of warranty, but awards fewer and fewer points for each extra year as the warranty approaches 10 years. Expressed in graphical terms, the curve representing quality points for increases in real quality rises steeply at the beginning and then flattens out towards the ceiling. This would actually make the quality score function resemble more closely a normal human utility curve:[1] the sixth portion of ice cream does not taste quite as well as the first, or having a bicycle with three more gears is more useful if it means going from three to six than it is when going from 21 to 24. The only thing to remember is that we must communicate this to firms as well, not only to be fair but also to receive tenders approaching optimal solutions at optimal prices. To do that, firms must know that, in fact, our evaluation curve will not be linear, because mid-range quality differences are more important to us than extra quality towards the maximum end. The only curve that really has to be linear is the curve of price-quality ratios, but this is only generated when relating quality, after its score is fixed, to the price, which does not have to be evaluated via a formula because the price is the price.

9.3. NON-BINARY QUALITATIVE CRITERIA

The third type of quality criterion is the one that is neither binary nor quantitative, but purely a matter of individual quality perception. "Aesthetic value" of a water tap could be one such criterion. A water tap can be more or less pretty, so it is not a binary criterion, and its looks cannot be measured in centimetres or volts or minutes, so it is not quantitative either. Still, it is perfectly legitimate for a contracting authority to state that it wants nice looking water taps, for example for representative premises at the city hall, and that the nicer they are, the more quality points it will give, meaning that nice looking taps can afford to be more expensive.

---

[1]   See Appendix II for a further discussion.

We have the impression that some procurers are uncomfortable with the subjectivity of such a criterion, but it is a reality. In fact, *almost everything* about tender specifications is subjective: from the subjective decision that we actually need water taps now, to the minimum technical requirement that the taps must be made of chrome-plated steel and conduct both cold and hot water and not just cold water. The fact that we are willing to pay extra if the tap has a handle for temperature regulation, rather than knobs, is just as legitimate as the other choices we have already made. The only thing that needs to be objectivized is the nature of our award criteria and the weighting. For example, we cannot suddenly say that the award goes to a tenderer who proposed a water tap that can be pulled out and turned into a hose, if this was mentioned nowhere, not even in general terms of functionality. But if we are willing to evaluate aesthetic appeal, then evidently this is what we find important, and this is what we will have to evaluate, for example on a scale of 0 to 10. Let us not forget that product positioning based on prestige, aesthetics and brand appeal is absolutely natural on the market. Suppliers often offer several product ranges that differ in functional but also in intangible aspects such as exclusivity, and we need to describe, in a human language, what range we are aiming for. The alternative is to describe the product we want by tailoring technical specifications to the desired brand, but that is unlawful – or at least it should be unlawful in case it is not – and it is in any event unfair and economically inefficient.

Still, how should we give points for something like aesthetics, on a scale of 0 to 10? As before, we should know what the minimum standard is and what the maximum usefulness is beyond which we refuse to spend any extra money. A water tap made of plastic is technically non-compliant; a simple normal tap with knobs is acceptable (zero extra points); a prettier one with knobs is better (4 out of 10); a nice one with a handle is perfect (10 out of 10). A tap made of solid gold, with diamonds on it, is also 10 out of 10, since it has already achieved maximum usefulness and we will not pay anything extra for diamonds. The price-quality ratio will take care of the rest, for if the luxury model is more expensive than the normal best quality, while their quality scores are equal, then the normal best quality will have a better ratio.

How to explain to firms what exactly we will find excessive, though? While it is normally illegal and, in terms of competition, inefficient to announce what brand we are seeking – this excludes all other brands or leads us to write overly specific tender specifications – it is often possible to use a descriptive term for a quality segment that is recognized on the market. This could be "mid-sized" or "D-segment" in the case of cars, "A" or "B" providers, "premium" or "generic" supplies. In addition, we recall that the weight of the price criterion itself is a powerful indicator for companies which market segment we are aiming for, and how they should position their tender in order to maximize their chances to win.

Again, let us be clear. Maximum quality is not the best imaginable quality in the universe. Nor is it the quality of the tender that happens to be the best among the tenders we received, because that would basically allow the tenderers to tell us what is good and what is bad. Instead, maximum quality is the best useful quality *that we are willing to pay for*. Every tender's quality score must stop growing at some point in the evaluation, and that point is when it stops adding useful quality that is worth more money to us. Think of the number of pizza toppings in a restaurant. We may accept paying €10 for a pizza margarita, another €2 if it has ham on it (first topping), and another €1 for additional onions (second topping). If the waiter offers us a third topping, we will not pay anything extra for it, because now it is enough. A pizza margarita is therefore our baseline acceptable minimum quality; our maximum useful quality, at which we stop paying extra for more, is two toppings. The quality score function is not linear in this case either, because the utility of each additional topping diminishes, the second being only half as valuable to us as the first.

9.4. POINT INFLATION

We turn to a phenomenon that we call point inflation, meaning that points are given without any good reason, either because we have to, or because we want to be nice to tenderers. If you realize that all tenders end up having the same quality score, it could be that all tenders really are near-identical in their quality, or that our evaluation grid forced us to give identical scores to everyone, as we will discuss shortly, but it could also mean that you have suffered point inflation.

For example, let us say we want to lease coffee machines for our office building, machines offering a nice variety of coffee types, and a service to keep the machines maintained and supplied with fresh coffee beans. We had specified in the tender documents as a selection criterion that any supplier must have a maintenance crew close by for repairs. In the technical specifications we had also stated that any beans must be fair-trade coffee. And we had said that for us coffee variety is an award criterion because we appreciate the ability to choose between different types of coffee. And now imagine we open and evaluate the quality of the first tender and we say the following: "So, let's give this firm 5 points for maintenance, because it has a technician who can react promptly and repair the machine. Another 10 points because the coffee is fairly traded, and we appreciate this fact. And as regards variety, well, there is coffee and cappuccino, so there is already *some* variety, so let's be nice and give them, say, 10 out of 20 points, and see whether it has espresso, too."

What just happened? What happened is that we just gave this firm 25 points for nothing. *Of course* it has a technician, that is why the firm got selected in the first place. And *of course* its coffee is fair-trade, otherwise it would not have been technically compliant. And why should we start the evaluation of coffee variety by giving everybody half the total points, as long as they offer more than one button? We recall that each quality point we give justifies a higher price. The more points tenderers collect on the quality front, the more they can afford to lose out on the price front, so the more expensive they can allow themselves to be. If our award criterion was "variety", then firms offering only one button should get eliminated for technical non-compliance (because there is no variety at all), and zero extra points for proposing two buttons (i.e. the most basic form of variety). Only once they start offering several types of latte macchiato should they start earning real quality points, because that is the real difference for which we are willing to pay extra.

The practical effect of point inflation, meaning the generous award of quality points already for basic quality or mere admissibility, is a compression of quality differences. All offers will end up with more or less the same quality score. When this happens, the only difference a firm can still make lies in the price. In the end, the lowest bidder, often offering the worst quality, wins.

The graphical representations below show the effect of quality compression. The first figure represents a simple lowest-bid award, where tenders are distributed on a single price axis. There is no quality axis, since in lowest-bid awards there is no competition on quality beyond technical specifications, only price competition. The second figure represents a price-quality award, with two axes. Prices, on the horizontal axis, are what they are; the quality scores on the vertical axis, however, depend on the way we translate actual quality into points, so the quality score for any given tender is actually a function of real quality. At first there is a relatively wide spread in quality scores. The winner is by definition the tender that offers the steepest quality increase given its price, in this case B. In the next scenario, all tenders are for whatever reason given the same quality score; B can no longer distinguish itself from A on its quality, since scores are equal for all, so A wins by default for being the cheapest. The way the tenders are arranged horizontally at a certain quality level as a result of quality compression resembles the way they are arranged on a single horizontal price axis in a lowest-bid award, where quality is fixed and where only the price decides.

Figure 18. Tenders on a price axis in a lowest-bid award

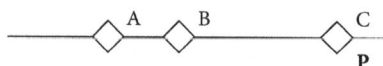

Figure 19. Tenders on a price and a quality axis in a price-quality award with a wide quality spread

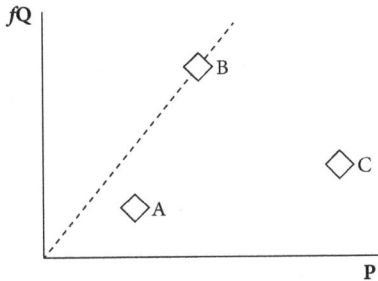

Figure 20. Tenders on a price and a quality axis in a price-quality award with a narrow quality spread

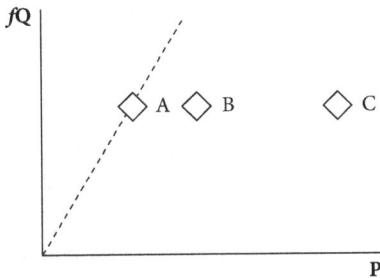

Turning price-quality awards effectively into lowest-bid awards through quality compression is undesirable for two reasons. First, we did not necessarily want to let the cheapest offer win, otherwise we would have opted for an actual lowest-bid award. Second, if high-quality suppliers had known that in the end the price would decide – since their quality score is basically the same as the score of cheap brands – then they could have saved themselves the trouble of making an offer in the first place, or they could have proposed a cheaper basic solution.

9.5. ASSESSMENT GRIDS

The second possible reason for distorted quality scores, apart from the human tendency to want to be nice to companies, are assessment grids that are too rigid. In principle, assessment grids are meant to help evaluators express their opinion on different quality aspects: they are essentially questionnaires. The problem is that some grids are split up into many tiny, almost mathematical segments. Can orders be placed online? Yes – 3 points; no 0 – points. Supplies are delivered within a week – 2 points; within two weeks – 1 point. Each additional engineer with a 10-year experience is worth 5 points, and so on. There may be sectors or features where the quality differences between possible tenders are very predictable and easily quantifiable. Yet sometimes it turns out that all tenders are more or less identical on one quality aspect – for which we had reserved lots of points – while the real difference between them lies somewhere else. As a result, all tenders will quickly reach the same high score, while the remaining point spread will not accurately reflect the real differences between them.

While it is important to be transparent, we must acknowledge that it is simply not always possible to guess in advance where the differences between tenders will lie. Say orders can be placed online, but the website is slow and confusing. Should such an offer really get the same 3 points as a well-designed platform, one that even has its own app for mobile devices, something we had not even thought of?

The EU Public Procurement Directive explicitly provides for a possibility to list award criteria in decreasing order of importance.[2] Even when it is possible to allocate points in advance on certain features, this should nonetheless allow evaluators to express their perception on a few broad categories, each with a sufficient range of points. Otherwise the evaluator may well find that, having added all the points for all the 200 sub-criteria, the total score does not at all reflect real quality perception. Transparency and predictability are not achieved by creating pseudo-science, as if all quality differences are purely and predictably mathematical. They are not. Transparency and predictability are much better achieved by announcing honestly what it is that we are looking for in an offer, by allowing evaluators sufficient space to distinguish basic quality from high quality, and by clearly explaining the reasons for the award decision to unsuccessful tenderers.

Might a court not annul our award decision if we are subjective in our evaluation? There are two things to bear in mind. First, there is a difference between expressing quality perception and being arbitrary. University lecturers routinely grade essays and theses, translating perceived quality under known quality standards – relevance of the topic, clarity of writing – into an overall numerical score. The risk of arbitrary grading is addressed by, for example, the duty to re-justify the grade in case of a complaint, or, in the case of theses, the involvement of a second reader or a whole committee to begin with. Similarly, tender evaluation committees, typically also including external members, are appointed to provide a collective assessment and attenuate individual preferences, while award decisions are normally subject to verification, review and audit. Second, regarding the risk of challenge in court for alleged subjectivity, we submit that we should be much more concerned about

---

2   Article 67 (5) of Directive 2014/24/EU.

annulment due to insufficient *reasons*: a table with simply a list of points and no comments, or with vague or generic comments that do not say anything about how exactly we arrived at our final judgment, truly exposes award decisions to the risk of annulment.[3] Even the most hyper-mathematical assessment grid with 200 sub-categories and bafflingly complex mathematical formulas cannot replace the simple and very fundamental duty to state reasons in a clear, honest, comprehensible and human language. And if the quality criterion is not quantitative, then this calls for an even greater effort to explain, in normal speech, why we assessed a tender in one way and not another.

---

[3] See cases T-264/06 *DC-Hadler*, T-272/06 *Evropaiki Dynamiki v. Court of Justice*, par. 43, T-465/04 *Evropaiki Dynamiki v. Commission*, T-461/08 *Evropaiki Dynamiki v. EIB*, T-57/09 *Alfastar*, T-300/07 *Evropaiki Dynamiki v. Commission*, par. 72, T-447/10 *Evropaiki Dynamiki v. Court of Justice*.

CHAPTER 10

CHOICE OF PROCEDURE

Depending on the nature and value of the contract to be awarded, national and European public procurement regimes typically provide for several possible procurement procedures. The contracting authority can in such case choose which procedure to follow in order to award a particular contract. In one type of procedure, for example, all tenders are received and opened at the same time, and the winner gets the award; in others, candidates are first pre-selected, and only those that get selected are invited to officially tender. This is irrespective of the award method – price, cost, or price-quality ratio – and instead has to do with the method of publishing the call and receiving tenders. Depending on the circumstances, different procedures have different advantages and drawbacks.

As regards high-value awards under EU procurement law, the most common procedures are the open procedure, the restricted procedure, as well as negotiated procedures including the competitive procedure with negotiation. Since national procurement laws differ between countries, we will not go into too much detail regarding the specifics of any of these types of procedure. What we can do, though, is to use these EU procedures as illustrations of broader classes of procedures and their underlying logic. Where national equivalents of these procedures exist, or where authorities in EU member states must actually choose from among the EU procedures themselves because the value of their contract exceeds the threshold of the EU Public Procurement Directive, our discussion might help make certain choices more explicit.

10.1. OPEN PROCEDURES

The most straightforward procedure under EU procurement law is the open procedure. Equivalents surely exist in any national regime. The idea is that the call for tenders is advertised – in the case of the EU this happens through a contract notice in the Official Journal, which is accessible online free of charge – and any interested firm can submit a tender. Tenders are opened, checked for technical and administrative compliance, exclusion, selection and award criteria, and the contract is awarded to the winner. What is distinctive about the open procedure and its national equivalents is that, first, everybody is free to tender, and that, second, no negotiations take place after the opening. The openness of the procedures means that tenderers are not pre-selected, so that the competition is literally open to anyone; and the absence of negotiations make the award a very immediate, almost automatic and therefore highly predictable act.

10.2. RESTRICTED PROCEDURES

Restricted procedures, by contrast, are two-stage procedures. The first stage is open, in the sense that a contract notice is published and anyone can submit a candidacy, meaning an application to be invited to submit a tender. The second stage is restricted, in that the contracting authority applies selection criteria to determine which companies are invited to submit an actual tender. The award is then made, again without negotiation, to the winning tenderer.

There are benefits, compared to the open procedure, for both the contracting authority and the firms. First, contracting authorities receive tenders only from firms which have already been selected, meaning firms that have sufficient financial and professional capacity, so they can focus on the merits of the tenders. Selection criteria, to put it simply, are a means to choose firms that we consider serious, and to reject firms that we would not want to work with because they are too small, too inexperienced, or too financially unstable for the contract we want to award. For firms, meanwhile, the pre-selection also has advantages. If a firm does not have enough capacity anyway, it is told so at an early stage, and can save itself the trouble of preparing a full tender. If the selection is carried out in the form of a ranking, selecting the five most capable firms for example, non-selected firms may equally save themselves the cost of tendering. Restricted procedures are therefore ideal in cases where the preparation of a tender is costly. We might think, for example, of a call for tenders for office furniture supplies, where tenderers must send samples of their furniture – desks and chairs and cupboards – transporting them by truck to a hangar for physical evaluation. Another example could be tenders for advanced research projects, the preparation of which already requires time and effort. Here it would normally be efficient to pre-select, and request tenders, and samples, only from those firms that meet financial and professional selection criteria.

The drawback is that restricted procedures are less open – that is why they are called restricted. If none of the pre-selected candidates actually tenders, we will never know if another firm might have presented a full offer at the very end in an open procedure. But on the substance restricted procedures are not much more restrictive than an open procedure: whether we select firms right at the start, like in a restricted procedure, or at the very end, like in an open one, selection does take place in any case.

As regards the time they take, restricted procedures are not necessarily more burdensome than open procedures either. True, procurement officers might hesitate to use a restricted procedure since they would have to allow for two periods, one for candidacies and one for actual tenders, which together are longer than the single period in open procedures. However, they are not *much* longer; in fact, if in open procedures we spend much time checking selection criteria and asking for clarifications from firms, an open procedure might even take longer overall. Besides, launching a contract notice under a restricted procedure also buys us some time, because while we wait for candidacies, we can still finalize the full technical specifications. These are, after all, only sent to selected firms.

Certain types of restricted procedures are actually much faster at the tendering stage in comparison to full procedures, namely restricted procedures that rely on a list of pre-selected candidates for whom admissibility is already confirmed, and from whom only substantive offers are requested. The classical solution is the call-for-interest list, which is a shortlist of candidates who had expressed their interest to be included in a database and who had their economic and financial capacity and their admissibility under exclusion criteria checked at the start. A technically more advanced solution is the dynamic purchasing system, where candidates in the database are requested to tender electronically for the quick awards of contracts for generic works or services and widely available off-the-shelf supplies.[1] The 2014 EU Public Procurement Directive seeks to make the dynamic purchasing system more attractive to contracting authorities, essentially by turning it from a type of open procedure into a type of restricted procedure. As a result, time is saved because admissibility verification is not carried out for each individual contract award but just once, when firms are accepted to the database, and continued admissibility is merely updated. The actual award, then, can focus on the content of tenders.

10.3. NEGOTIATED PROCEDURES

The third major types of procedures are those that allow for negotiations after the opening of tenders. Under EU law these are known as negotiated procedures where no contract notice is published, and so-called competitive procedures with negotiation, formerly known as negotiated procedures with contract notice. The difference is that, in the first case, the contracting authority contacts companies directly, and asks them to tender, without the mandatory publicity of a contract notice. Above EU thresholds, meaning in high-value awards, this is allowed only in exceptional cases.[2] In the second version, the authority

---

[1]   Article 34 of Directive 2014/24/EU.

[2]   Article 32 of Directive 2014/24/EU.

publishes a contract notice to receive candidacies from firms that request to be invited to tender.[3] What both negotiated procedures have in common is that, unlike open and restricted procedures, they allow the contracting authority to discuss with the tenderers in order to adjust the price and quality of their initial tenders. Tenderers may therefore make follow-up offers. Thus, the firm that would have won initially is not necessarily the final winner, because another firm can improve its offer even more.

Negotiated procedures can provoke mixed feelings. On the one hand, they can be perceived as suspect, since they involve bargaining that can be highly intransparent, and since they can allow for the pre-targeting of firms to be contacted in the first place. Especially when publicity is weak or absent, the risk of favouritism and abuse seems high. This is why the EU Public Procurement Directive insists on contract notices, with narrow exceptions, such as when we are dealing with a monopolist so there is no competition anyway.

On the other hand, though, negotiated procedures provide for a flexibility and user-friendliness that open and restricted procedures cannot match. In fact, the availability of negotiation makes the procedure come very close to what is perfectly normal in private buying.[4] When we buy a kitchen for our new home, for example, we would normally not sit down alone at home, write down exactly what we think we want, and then walk with that description into different stores, buying only what matches our own idea. Rather, we would request an offer for a standard kitchen of our preferred style, and then sit down with the salesperson to discuss the details. More or less the same should be possible when buying a kitchen for the canteen of a government building. Negotiations are after all there to achieve, starting from an initial offer, an even better match between supply and demand. It is not simply price bargaining. Earlier we used the example of the purchase of theft detection gates at the exit of a library that include an alarm counter. If we receive offers from three tenderers, we might as well ask them whether the gates are also available with chrome edges, or in plexiglas instead of normal plastic, possibly at the original price. Or we might ask them how much we could save off the price if we leave out the alarm counter.[5]

The 2014 reform of the EU Public Procurement Directive makes negotiated procedures with contract notice much more widely available, in a broader effort to meet authorities' need for greater flexibility. Tellingly, the procedure is no longer called "exceptional". Instead, it is a standard procedure for cases where, for example, off-the-shelf solutions are not suitable and products must be adapted to specific needs. Since the procedure requires the publication of a contract notice, it basically has the full publicity of an open procedure, but with

---

[3]   Article 29 of Directive 2014/24/EU.
[4]   See also K. Krüger, 'Ban-on-Negotiations in Tender Procedures: Undermining the Best Value for Money', in K. Thai, ed., *International Handbook of Public Procurement*, Boca Raton: CRC Press 2009.
[5]   See also Chapter 5.6 on negotiations.

the added flexibility of a negotiated one. We stress that negotiated procedures do require a diligent approach to honesty and transparency, with due regard for the principle of equal treatment of tenderers. Yet if this is observed, procedures with negotiation provide us with much more freedom to seek, in a highly efficient manner, either the lowest price or the most value for money.

We add that negotiated procedures can also be arranged as two-stage processes, or as procedures with even more stages. The idea is then to request initial tenders from everyone, negotiate and request follow-up tenders from the best, and, where applicable, negotiate again and obtain a final offer from, say, the last two firms. While the two-stage restricted procedure is meant to reject companies with insufficient capacity, multi-stage negotiated procedures can, in addition, be used to weed out firms that do have enough capacity, but whose tender quality is too low or whose price is too high from the start. In principle this makes sense if contracting authorities are flooded with too many tenders, or if negotiations are technically too complex, so that they do not want to waste their time with too many separate negotiations. If we receive tenders from just five or six firms in normal procurement, though, we might as well keep talking to all of them.

10.4. EXCEPTIONAL PROCEDURES

Depending on the legal system at hand, exceptional procedures may exist that typically involve shorter deadlines, less competition and less publicity than ordinary procurement procedures do. In the case of high-value awards governed by EU procurement law, these are the negotiated procedures without contract notice. Thus, a contracting authority may argue that recourse to such an exceptional procedure is necessary because of urgency, or because for technical reasons there is anyway only one company that can provide the necessary goods or services so there is no point in starting a competitive procedure. These questions have to be resolved case by case, of course. It may be true that there is a real urgency, because a roof collapsed and we need a contractor to stabilize and rebuild it; or that we are renting space at a particular airport, so obviously there is only one possible provider, namely that airport. But EU law at least is relatively critical of contracting authorities trying to invoke exceptional circumstances to justify less competitive procedures.[6] And so are we. For example, if it is our own fault because we waited too long with our call for tenders, then this does not count as urgency; if we simply find a particular provider very convenient, for example because the firm already works for us, then this does not necessarily

---

6   See cases 199/85 *Commission v. Italy*, par. 14, C-57/94 *Commission v. Italy*, C-601/10 *Commission v. Greece*, C-20/01 *Commission v. Germany*, par. 66, C-318/94 *Commission v. Germany*, C-24/91 *Commission v. Spain*, par. 14, C-107/92 *Commission v. Italy*.

mean that it has an actual monopoly. Choosing the right procedure can help us make a more efficient award; where exceptional procedures exist, they are meant for exceptional circumstances. For example, we very much encourage buyers to use competitive dialogues, and thus receive input from potential suppliers, to improve the quality of their tender specifications in the case of complex contracts. However, exceptional procedures are not meant to help contracting authorities systematically avoid competitive tendering.[7]

Where exceptional procedures do apply and are used, notably where competition is limited to very few or just a single company, we should apply more, not less caution in awarding the contract. The reason is that, in case of a single tender, that tender will automatically be the economically most advantageous, because by definition it offers the lowest purchase price, entails the lowest costs, and presents the best price-quality ratio among the tenders received. Since tender content cannot be compared to a wider range of competing solutions if there are too few offers, and since it cannot be compared to other offers at all if there is only one, it becomes particularly important to bear in mind the buyer's thresholds of acceptability, and to negotiate where permitted and where necessary. In other words, it would be unwise to relax, accept any price that is within budget or that is close to prices from previous contracts, and quickly declare the tendering stage over. Instead, preliminary market research and bargaining must replace what would usually be done during the evaluation of several competitive tenders in a normal award. Where competitors cannot serve as benchmarks with respect to each other, the contracting authority needs to fix benchmarks of its own, such as target prices and a target price-quality ratio. It needs to do that in any case, of course, even when there are many tenders; but when there are *not* many tenders, it becomes vital to define and apply benchmarks with even greater rigour.

---

[7]   See also Chapter 13 on anti-abuse safeguards.

CHAPTER 11

THE POST-AWARD STAGE

The central part of the procurement process is concluded with the award decision. Often an award notice must be published, so that not only the call for tenders but also its outcome is made publicly available,[1] or contracting authorities must publish regular reports or lists of awardees. The winning tenderer is informed of the result, while unsuccessful tenderers are informed of the reasons for their rejection. Meanwhile, for the contract performance, the award is only the beginning. Lessons learned at the tendering stage, and during contract performance, should in turn feed into the next call for tenders.

11.1. THE DUTY TO STATE REASONS

One of the most unpleasant things, from a procurement officer's point of view, is when a rejected tenderer files a complaint or a court action against an award decision. But we should remember that, from a company's point of view, being rejected is not a pleasant experience either. To stay open and transparent during the post-award stage as well, our information to rejected tenderers should be clear and well-reasoned.

According to EU case-law, the duty to state reasons is not a duty to start a philosophical exercise on why one offer was successful and another was not. In fact, the duty to state reasons is there for unsuccessful tenderers to know the reasons of their rejection so that they can effectively defend their rights in court, and so that the court can exercise judicial review.[2] As a result, the duty to state reasons is fulfilled if the tenderer clearly understood why he or she got rejected.[3] Contracting authorities are not obliged to give the full version of the evaluation report,[4] or to disclose confidential parts of it,[5] or to comment on

---

[1]   For example Article 75 (2) of Directive 2014/24/EU.
[2]   See for example case T-183/10 *Sviluppo Globale*, T-169/00 *Esedra*.
[3]   C-629/11 *Evropaiki Dynamiki v. Commission*.
[4]   C-462/10 *Evropaiki Dynamiki v. EEA*, C-561/10 *Evropaiki Dynamiki v. Commission*, C-629/11 *Evropaiki Dynamiki v. Commission*, T-488/12 *Citeb and Belgo-Metal v. European Parliament*.
[5]   T-514/09 *bpost*.

every little detail of the evaluation,[6] or to start a lengthy discussion with unsuccessful firms.[7]

Still, it is only fair, and in fact in our economic interest, to be straightforward with rejected firms. A good explanation is more easily accepted, and may make the firm less likely to file a complaint. For example, it surely helps if the reasons for the rejection are explained immediately, right in the rejection letter, without making firms ask for further details. If a firm feels that we treat it decently, it may come back and participate in future calls for tenders as well.

11.2. EVALUATION AND FOLLOW-UP

In the case of recurring contracts, but also in the case of series of similar contracts, procurement resembles a cycle. At least it should, in that lessons from the past should be incorporated in future calls for tenders and in the continuously improved procurement process.

If the first call for tenders did not lead to an award, what was the reason? If no-one tendered, or if a firm that we had expected to tender did not show up, we should certainly be interested in why that was. So go and ask them, give them a call, write them an e-mail. After the conclusion of the call for tenders we are, after all, again free to communicate normally with economic operators. Why did they not tender? Were they simply too busy? Did they find certain elements in the call unacceptable? Perhaps they could not accept our general conditions, or could not provide what we had specified, or could not offer a warranty like we had prescribed, or the penalties we had foreseen were unacceptable to them? Or perhaps they saw our selection criteria and decided that it was not worth the effort to tender? Of perhaps they felt, reading the technical specifications, that the call was clearly tailored to suit one particular firm, so they assumed that the game was rigged? Or perhaps they simply had not heard of the call? All these pieces of information are relevant, because they allow us to draft and advertise our next call for tenders in a better, more inviting, and more market-oriented way.

Meanwhile, even if our call for tenders *was* successful, we should keep an eye on the performance of the contractor. By "we", we mean chiefly the operational services but also the ordinary users of the goods and services in question. If the contractor turns out to make too many mistakes and to show lack of capacity or professionalism, perhaps next time we can sharpen our selection criteria; if it turns out that the contract does not cover certain extra services that would have been desirable, then next time we might put them into our award criteria. If there is constant haggling over the meaning of a contract clause, our next

---

[6] C-629/11 *Evropaiki Dynamiki v. Commission.*
[7] T-211/07 *AWWW*, par. 43, T-407/07 *CMB Maschinenbau*, par. 177.

contract should be clearer. And if, in the case of long-term contracts, the market has meanwhile been producing innovations, meaning that our old contract terms are no longer competitive, then this is an occasion to not prolong the contract and to launch a new call for tenders with a view to obtaining the newly available market solutions.

Constant quality management and evaluation of the performance of contractors, as part of the supply chain or otherwise, is absolutely natural in the private sector, but it is no less applicable to public clients. In the public procurement cycle, at least three types of evaluations should be carried out routinely:

- Evaluation of the current *contractor*, with a view to prolonging or discontinuing the contract, to terminating it, to imposing penalties, or to paying out satisfaction bonuses if this has been foreseen in the contract. The main questions are how responsive and reliable the contractor company is, whether it meets deadlines and fulfils quality, social and environmental standards, how well it cooperates with other contractors, how well it manages its subcontractors, whether internal clients using the goods or services – staff members, politicians, citizens – are satisfied, etc.
- Evaluation of the current *contract*, for example at half-time, with a view to prolonging or discontinuing it, in the light of technological change and other developments in the market. The main question is whether our current contract conditions are still competitive and economically efficient in comparison to what has become available on the market since the contract was awarded. If not, this may be reason to discontinue it, and launch a new call with a view to profiting from newly available solutions, lower prices, etc.
- Evaluation of the *tender specifications*, before launching a call for a successor contract. The main questions are whether the conditions from the previous call for tenders are still applicable, whether there are conditions that were particularly satisfactory, whether there were conditions that caused problems at either the tendering or the performance stage, whether some clauses are unusual or burdensome in comparison with normal market conditions and might prevent firms from tendering, etc. Feedback from the existing contractor and from firms who had not responded to the previous call, even though we had expected to see them, is particularly vital.

Quality assessment not only helps us manage our contractors once they have won the award: already the simple fact that monitoring and evaluation, customer satisfaction surveys, penalties, bonuses, regular meetings with the manager, or an escape clause in case of poor quality are foreseen in the call for tenders sends a message to firms. This does not have to be presented in a threatening way, simply as a clarification that the client attaches great importance to quality. The planning stage of a call for tenders is, in that logic, not a completely fresh start but rather a stage in which lessons from evaluations of past calls for tenders are integrated.

CHAPTER 12

GREEN PROCUREMENT

Since government spending typically constitutes a considerable share of GDP, public authorities as clients can promote certain policy goals through the way they procure goods and services. In the case of environmental protection, green procurement can help create general demand for environmentally friendly solutions through the government's own demand. More indirectly, public authorities can set a good example for society in not just prescribing greener standards for businesses and consumers, but in buying green themselves. Green procurement is essentially public buying in which environmental considerations explicitly play a role,[1] for example:

- The *technical specifications* may insist that the needed supplies must comply with ambitious environmental standards, or be certified with eco-labels. In fact the very object of the procurement can be green already, for example if we are leasing a hybrid car, buying emission rights, or improving the thermal insulation of our government building.
- The *selection criteria* may insist that having an environmental audit scheme like EMAS or ISO 14001 forms part of the technical and professional competence of tendering firms. In other words, even when the object of the procurement is not particularly green, in any case companies must have mechanisms in place to reduce waste, for example.
- The *award criteria* may include environmental aspects as quality criteria. For example, supplies may receive extra quality points if they are made of recycled materials or if they are biodegradable. This means that we accept that tenders offering such greener products may be more expensive than tenders that are less green. Quality criteria are there precisely to justify higher prices if what is offered is something that we appreciate.

To foster awareness for the environmental dimension of public buying, it can be helpful to qualify certain contract awards as being green to different degrees, and to compile statistics on the share of green procurement. It is not enough,

---

[1] See, for toolkits, recommendations and documentation for public buyers, the Green Public Procurement website of the European Commission at ec.europa.eu/environment/gpp/index_ en.htm.

however, to always include a standard green award criterion by default, because the environmental aspect can manifest itself in different forms, and it may in some cases be simply inapplicable.

CHAPTER 13

MANAGING THE RISK OF IRREGULARITIES AND INEFFICIENCIES

Why is public procurement so heavily regulated? The answer to that is given every time we open the newspaper, and read that somewhere some mayor has been giving public road building contracts to a construction company that belonged to his brother-in-law. Public procurement means the spending of public money, and this must happen in an efficient way, and certainly not in a way that serves private interests at the expense of the taxpayer. Hence the insistence on transparency, equal treatment of tenderers, and non-discrimination in the award of public contracts. Hence also the obligation to publish contract notices and award decisions; hence the right for tenderers to be physically present to witness the opening of envelopes in open procedures; and hence the obligation to fix award criteria in advance and not afterwards.

13.1. IRREGULARITIES IN PUBLIC PROCUREMENT

In the case of the mayor and his brother-in-law, the problem may have been simple corruption, where a tenderer actually gives or promises money or other favours to the official in order to receive a public contract. Or it may have been a more fundamental conflict of interests, where an economic, emotional, or other link to a tenderer – in this case family – compromises the official's objectivity. As a result, the contracting authority misses out on potentially better prices, or better quality, or both, that might have been obtained from a different firm, since already a particular firm had been favoured from the beginning for unrelated reasons. This is problematic from an efficiency point of view – apart from the fact that conflicts of interest are illegal, that their presence can lead to the annulment of an award decision, and that even the failure to investigate indications for a conflict of interest can be unlawful.[1]

However, we presume that the most common form of irregularities and other types of economic inefficiency in public procurement has nothing to do with criminal intent or deliberate favours within the family. It is rather inadequate

---

[1]   T-160/03 *AFCon*, par. 91.

procurement design and control mechanisms,[2] or pure habit: the tendency to keep calling the same firms, or the tendency to want to keep the current contractor company because it is just fine. Yet while this is a human explanation, it does not mean it is efficient or acceptable.[3]

13.2. THE INEFFICIENCY OF REDUCED COMPETITION

Someone might perhaps argue that sticking with the "usual suspects" in local public procurement actually is economically efficient. After all, dealing only with known firms reduces the risk of ending up with bad firms, and changing from one contractor to another can entail costs as well. We do not agree with this logic, though, and continue to call for openness and open-mindedness in public procurement. Sticking with usual suspects is *not* economically efficient, chiefly because it creates overall costs to society and hidden costs to ourselves. Costs to society are called negative externalities, meaning costs that are not borne by the one who causes them, but by society. If people feel that government contracts are basically shared between a few established companies, so it makes no sense to even write a tender, then this works against entrepreneurship and market efficiency. Hidden costs to ourselves arise if newcomers are blocked or discouraged, so we will never know how much public money we could have saved, or how much extra quality we could have obtained for that public money. Thus, if we do not want to deal with bad firms, we should design appropriate selection criteria, learning from previous contracts, not just exclude everyone we do not know. If the cost of changing contractors is high, we should openly make switching costs a part of the price schedule, or award long-term contracts, but following a fair and competitive procurement. And if the usual suspects really *are* that good, then they should have no problem winning in an open, honest, and well-designed call for tenders.

13.3. RISK MANAGEMENT AND CONTINUOUS IMPROVEMENT OF THE PROCUREMENT PROCESS

To manage any strategic process, it is essential to manage its risks. For the proper functioning of public procurement, a risk is any factor that prevents a public contract from being awarded to the tender offering the best value for money,

---

2   OECD, *Integrity in Public Procurement*, Paris: OECD 2007.
3   See also PWC EU Services / Utrecht University, *Public procurement: Costs we pay for corruption*, 2013.

meaning the successful tender emerging from the economically most efficient competition and proposing and implementing the economically most efficient solution. A conflict of interests on the part of the procurement officer is clearly such a risk, but, like we said, there are many more.

In order to take stock of existing risks and prioritize countermeasures for any given contracting authority or type of procurement or specific contract, we propose to draw up a "risk heat map". This is an inventory of the possible risks, allowing contracting authorities to focus on "hotspots" where risks are either most likely, or where their impact would be gravest if they came true, or both. In cases where technical specifications are drafted by an external planning bureau, while the particular sector in the region is rife with collusion between companies, for example, attention should be dedicated to possible conflicts of interest on the part of the bureau.

First, it is necessary to reflect on the *stages* of the procurement process at which risks may materialize. These are notably planning and needs analysis, the drafting of the call for tenders, the tendering, selection, evaluation and award stage, the performance and the closure and ex post evaluation. Second, it is necessary to identify the *origin* of the risk:[4] the external environment, such as flaws in or subsequent changes to applicable legislation; the system design such as procurement strategy, financial validation circuits and archiving; organization and people, such as staff qualification, habits and internal practices, inter-service cooperation and the confidentiality of documents; legality and regularity, such as absence of a clear interpretation of legislation, as well as fraud and collusion; and subject-specific origins regarding the legal and quality parameters of the contract. Having reflected on the stage and origin of risks, the contracting authority can estimate the gravity of the impact and the probability of the impact of the risk, for instance on a scale of one to five. Including both impact and probability in a matrix allows risk managers to focus control measures on "hotspots", where one multiplied by the other is highest:

Figure 21. Example of a risk probability-impact matrix

Impact \ Probability	Very Low	Low	Medium	High	Certain
Critical					
High					
Medium					
Low					
Very Low					

---

4   European Commission, *Risk Management in the Commission, Implementation Guide*, internal document of the European Commission, version November 2013, Annex 1.

The reason why control measures must be prioritized is that they entail a cost as well. Some risks must be tackled irrespective of the cost effectiveness of the control, such as formal compliance with legislation. Others, however, require targeting in line with risk tolerance, meaning the acceptable level of risks. It is not very efficient to immediately impose heavy verification on each and every detail of procurement, because this disproportionately slows down the process and may easily turn into a formalistic routine of ticking boxes on a checklist. Instead, constant improvement to the quality of our procurement processes may make us less risk tolerant over time, allowing us at some point to start addressing the remaining low-impact, low-probability risks. Since these improvements result from past evaluations, including peer review and audits, they form part of a continuous improvement cycle known in quality management as PDCA:[5]

Figure 22. Continuous quality improvement (PDCA) cycle

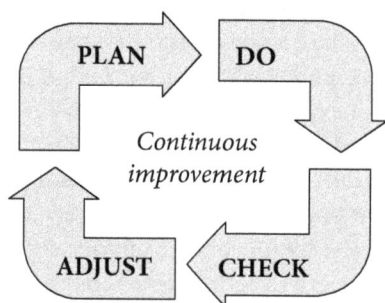

13.4. PROCUREMENT RISKS AND RISK RESPONSE

The following indicative list summarizes potential risks in public procurement. Again, we focus not on deliberate bid-rigging, but rather on the many mundane risks that decrease efficiency:

- The need for the call for tenders is not clearly defined, or it is not justified from an economic or operational point of view, and unnecessary or sub-optimal purchases are made;
- A contract with a similar scope already exists;
- Preparation of the tender documents is not preceded by market research;
- Harder forms of openness are avoided by splitting up a big contract into several low-value awards, each made under less competitive procedures;[6]

---

5   R.D. Moen & C.L. Norman, 'Circling Back: Clearing up myths about the Deming cycle and seeing how it keeps evolving', *Quality Progress*, November 2010, p. 22–28.
6   See cases C-16/98 *Commission v. France* and C-574/10 *Commission v. Germany*.

- The contract is not divided into lots, so only the biggest firms can compete for it because only they have the means to cover all of it;
- In procedures where a limited number of firms must be invited to participate, the favoured firm is contacted, while the others are ill-suited alibi firms, so only the favoured firm will tender;
- Restrictions on the number of tenderers, for example in exceptional negotiated procedures, are invoked even if the call could have been opened to broader competition, for example by claiming that the current contractor is the only one who can carry out a new task;[7]
- Following an abortive openly competitive procedure, a less competitive procedure is launched but on different terms than the previous one;[8]
- New awards are given by significantly amending or extending existing contracts, rather than by launching a new call for tenders;[9]
- Contract clauses create monopolistic situations ("lock-in") or other entry barriers for future competitors, for example by granting long-term exclusive rights such as continued maintenance to the initial supplier, by leaving property rights with the contractor, or by not providing for removal or system migration by the contractor at the end of the contract;
- Conflicts of interests or inefficient habits exist, with the result that technical specifications, selection or, to a lesser extent, award criteria are tailored to the specifics of one particular firm or brand, so all others are disadvantaged or excluded, and that evaluation is biased;
- The price schedule does not list accurate consumption estimates; as a result, a favoured firm can give rebates on items that it knows will never be ordered, inflate prices for items that it knows will be ordered in great quantities, and/ or use economies of scale to give lower unit prices when it knows that actual consumption will be greater than announced;
- A mandatory but unnecessary visit to the premises favours local firms and creates a risk of collusion and of suboptimal tendering if the identity of interested firms is disclosed;
- Geographical proximity is invoked to justify a less competitive special procedure;[10]
- Deadlines are too short, so companies that had been informally pre-informed are at an advantage;
- Deadlines are shortened, evaluations and awards are hurried, and lowest-bid procedures instead of price-quality awards are launched due to short-term constraints at individual unit level, without sufficient regard to overall procurement strategy ("silo approach");

---

7   See cases C-199/85 *Commission v. Italy*, par. 14, C-57/94 *Commission v. Italy*, C-601/10 *Commission v. Greece*.

8   See case C-84/03 *Commission v. Spain*, par. 49.

9   See case C-454/06 *Pressetext* and Article 72 of Directive 2014/24/EU.

10   See case C-20/01 *Commission v. Germany*, par. 66.

- Urgency clauses are invoked to justify less competitive procedures;[11]
- Selection and award criteria, the weighting of award criteria and technical specifications are poorly designed, or adopted without a proper reflection on actual risks and needs, which lead to a mismatch between supply and demand and further risks during the performance phase;
- Excessively high expectations – such as selection criteria that favour the biggest firms, specifications that are out of proportion to the budget, contract clauses that are onerous and unusual in the market – or unnecessary bureaucratic barriers to participation result in the reception of no or very few relevant tenders;
- In price-quality awards, evaluation grids are designed in such way that everyone ends up with the same quality score, so only the price is left to decide, and pre-informed firms know that they should tender with their cheapest product, or the grids advantage heavily one particular solution without any actual benefit to the contracting authority;
- Regulatory formalities, such as publicity, restricted communication with firms between the call and the opening, simultaneous opening and deadlines, are not respected;
- An excessively high proportion of subcontracting, with weak control over subcontractors, allows for the effective award of contracts to ineligible or otherwise problematic firms;
- Unprofessional evaluation of tenders due to lack of adequate skills or methodology result in arbitrary evaluation results and a poorly justified evaluation report, exposing the contracting authority in case of litigation and leading to sub-optimal contract performance;
- Insufficient monitoring and contractual enforcement arrangements mean that the contractor's performance is no longer linked to the award decision;
- Experience from previous award procedures and contracts are insufficiently fed into new procedures, and no routine exists for continuous improvement of the procurement process involving all strategic actors;
- Different key actors – procurement officers, managers, verifiers, authorizing officers – are involved too late in the procurement process, and the head of procurement is not involved in strategic procurement planning and in early decisions on important contracts.

Once the risks are known, it is necessary to define an adequate risk response, or control measures that will prevent them. Some of the risks are already addressed by applicable legislation and internal administrative procedures, such as the mandatory involvement of evaluators and validators who are not hierarchically

---

[11] See cases C-199/85 *Commission v. Italy*, par. 14, C-57/94 *Commission v. Italy*, C-318/94 *Commission v. Germany*, C-24/91 *Commission v. Spain*, par. 14, C-107/92 *Commission v. Italy*, par. 13.

subordinated to the authorizing officer. Additional measures may include an independent validation of expenditure at a centralized level, and a stricter segregation of duties between the drafter of calls and the evaluator of tenders. General procurement policy and essential elements of individual awards, such as selection criteria and the weighting of award criteria, may even be decided independently of the drafters, by a strategic procurement board at the level of top management. Yet sometimes the risk response cannot be straightforward, and requires above all gradual awareness raising, exchange, peer review and professional training. This is notably the case where the problem is not compliance with rules, but where sound financial management calls for diligence, flexibility, creativity and realism on the part of those involved in procurement design and the tendering process.

It is true that the publicity of calls for tenders on its own can deter corruption or other conflicts of interests or mundane inefficiencies, in that it becomes more important to pay attention and harder to brazenly favour certain firms. In that sense civil society, the media and unsuccessful tenderers are important actors in the enforcement of decent procurement. However publicity is typically an ex post measure: when the award decision is published, the procurement is already concluded; when the contract notice or the contract itself is published, the tender specifications have already been written. We must stress that the most dangerous form of inefficiency is the one that is hardest to detect, and it happens at the drafting stage. It reminds us of the Pareto principle, holding that 80% of problems result from 20% of causes. Applied to public procurement, we suggest that if the tendering stage represents 20% of the time and effort in a public contract's lifespan, then procurement design merits 80% of our attention.[12] Gains from improved efficiency through intelligent drafting are, in that case, considerable.

---

[12]   See P. Jouannet, *Techniques de négociation dans l'achat public, niveau 2* (training material), Paris: ACP 2014, p. 7.

CHAPTER 14
CONCLUSIONS

For most of this book we concentrated on the economic dimension of public buying. Thus, we kept reminding procurement officers that they are not only civil servants but also party to a market transaction, and that the point of this market transaction is to check the market, invite sellers, and make a good deal. However, it is true that procurement officers are also, to a great extent, anti-corruption officers. The typical setup is that technicians from an operational service define their needs and then contact their procurement specialist, or a centralized procurement service or agency, to launch a call for tenders, to be checked under some form of four-eye financial verification before authorization. If internal safeguards against abuse or mundane inefficiency are to be effective, they should set in right in these early stages. Is the assessment grid sufficiently open? Are selection criteria related to an actual risk, or are they needlessly excluding many firms for no reason? Are deadlines long enough, can a mandatory visit to the premises be avoided? Are consumption estimates reasonable, or is the quantity for each item simply "1"? Do the tender documents define the needs of the contracting authority, or are they already describing a particular solution? Is the call open enough, or is it designed to address only a few firms or even a single firm?

Diligent drafting of calls for tenders, and internal verification and validation procedures, cannot all be summarized into a fixed catalogue of dos and don'ts. They require a clear-headed approach to identify the risks of any particular design choice in a procurement procedure, as every procedure is different and presents its own challenges. Most inefficiencies are probably not due to any actual criminal schemes, but due to the inadequacy of certain habits. Often it is enough to simply ask "why". Why do you suggest these selection criteria? Why do you insist on so and so many millimetres, volts, litres or seconds in your technical specifications? Why did you make this or that an award criterion? If this is your proposed award criteria weighting, are you really willing to pay this much on that quality aspect?

We hope that our book helps procurement officers ask the right questions, and that it helps contracting authorities as a whole to invite free and fair competition, make efficient awards, and obtain good quality for their money. For actually it is not *their* money, it is taxpayer money. Public procurement officers are, in this context, both civil servants managing public affairs and economic operators buying goods and services on the market. Both aspects are important. A procurement officer who forgets that he or she is handling public affairs risks getting entangled in private interests; an officer who forgets that he or she is also a market participant may become too bureaucratic over the years. In our view, good procurement means that we are serving the public interest, and that we do this in a frank, transparent and straightforward way, leading to fair and efficient awards of public contracts.

APPENDIX I

THE ASSESSMENT OF THE ECONOMIC VIABILITY OF COMPANIES

As is the case with any selection criterion, the assessment of the economic health of companies as part of their financial standing is meant as a risk response. Where the bankruptcy of a contractor constitutes a significant risk for the performance of the contract and the continuity of overall operations, financial health can be imposed as a selection criterion. Normally this particular risk is significant where the contract has a long duration – which in accounting terms means over one year – and where the contractor is not easy to replace, with delays resulting in unacceptable damage to business continuity or the contracting authority's reputation. The purpose of the imposition of the health criterion is to lower the risk of contractor bankruptcy by evaluating tenders only from companies which meet this selection criterion, and to discard tenders from companies which do not. Yet this risk response has its own costs as well, in that it creates an additional admissibility criterion for tenderers and thereby restricts competition. That is why the financial health criterion, like any other selection criterion, should be appropriate in the light of the nature of the contract, proportionate to the risk, and non-discriminatory.

1. THE PROBABILITY OF BANKRUPTCY

Once it is established that financial health is a necessary selection criterion, the challenge is to find a method to estimate as accurately as possible the likelihood that a company will become bankrupt in the near future. This method must enable us to reject companies with a high risk and to select companies that are in good health. The risk of an inaccurate assessment method is that we let through companies whose bankruptcy probability is high, that we needlessly reject viable firms, or both. The first is a risk to contract performance. The rejection of healthy firms, meanwhile, is a risk to fair competition and market efficiency. And it is especially perfidious because we will probably never even get to see the tenders of firms which, having seen the relevant criterion in the call for tenders, realize that they are not eligible to obtain the contract anyway.

Some traditionally used criteria do have that distortive effect, though, if the financial health criterion is applied on the basis of any single, isolated financial indicator. Proper financial analysis employs a whole *range* of indicators to form a judgment on a company's viability: operating earnings, net earnings, gross cash flow, net profit margin, working capital, capital-to-turnover ratio, the ratio of turnover to total assets, net cash flows, etc.

None of them will justify, on its own, an informed viability assessment. An entire set of indicators must be applied, which is exactly what other actors do who are, like contracting authorities, interested in a firm's viability: venture capital investors, prospective long-term contractors including suppliers, credit insurers and factoring companies, and obviously banks that give loans to firms and must estimate their risk of default. We advocate using in public procurement a simplified tool that is also used by financial analysts for the same purposes: financial scoring.[1]

A financial score is nothing else but the result of a formula combining several accounting variables or ratios with different coefficients to produce a single number that measures corporate financial health. These coefficients reflect the impact that different indicators statistically have on bankruptcy risk. They are the result of a statistical technique called discriminant analysis, which allows drawing a line between sets of statistical data, in this case a large sample of financial accounts of companies that later did or did not go bankrupt. The selection criterion can then be a certain threshold of probability, above which the risk is too high, or a combination of such a threshold with other indicators.

It is important to stress that the scoring method, although it is more complex than the reliance on a single indicator, does not restrict but in fact opens up competition. The reason is that healthy firms which, for some explicable reason, would not meet an isolated-indicator criterion like positive net earnings, and that therefore would in such case not even bother to tender, can nevertheless tender if they know that their viability will be assessed in a way that captures much more accurately the truth.

Figure 23. Correlation between low risk of bankruptcy and an acceptable result of scoring or a single indicator

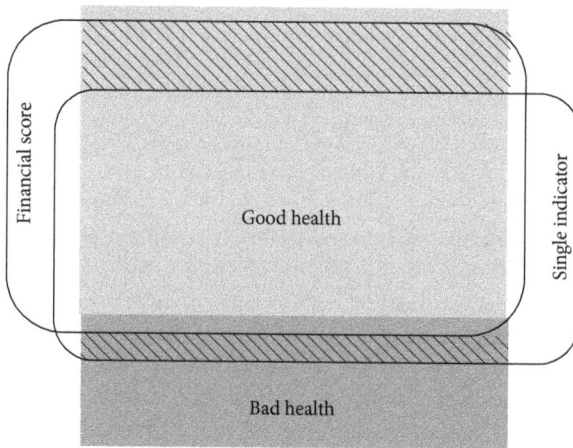

---

[1]   See E.I. Altman, 'Revisiting Credit Scoring Models in a Basel II Environment', in: M.K. Ong, ed., *Credit Ratings: Methodologies, Rationale and Default Risk*, London: Risk Books 2002, pp. 151–168; E.I. Altman, *Predicting Financial Distress Of Companies: Revisiting The Z-Score And Zeta* Models*, NYU Working Paper, July 2000; L. Mandru et al., 'The diagnosis of bankruptcy risk using score function', in: *Proceedings of the 9th WSEAS international conference on artificial intelligence, knowledge engineering and data bases (AIKED'10)*, Stevens Point: WSEAS 2010, pp. 83–87; J. Conan & M. Holder, *Variables explicatives de performance et contrôle de gestion dans les P.M.I.*, Paris: CERG, Université Paris Dauphine 1979.

No financial assessment, in fact no selection criterion in principle, can be 100% accurate. In order to approach 100% accuracy on a company's financial health we would probably need to go there, observe, and talk to a great number of company insiders for several months. This will be neither feasible nor cost-effective in ordinary procurement. However the accuracy of scoring in comparison to any isolated indicator is in any event considerable. Practitioners using scoring are invited to test on past awards how many selected firms they would have had to reject based on a single indicator; practitioners who use single indicators, and who did experience a contractor's bankruptcy in the past, are invited to check whether they would still have selected that firm had they used scoring at the time. And still, bankrupt contractors are visible, and we can count them; what we do not see are healthy firms which do not even tender because our financial selection criteria are too blunt and exclude them for no proper reason.

2. THE CONAN AND HOLDER SCORE

The Conan and Holder scoring method has been elaborated by two French economists, Joël Conan and Michel Holder, on the basis of a sample of small and medium-sized enterprises that are in general most vulnerable with regard to financial distress risks. It has the advantage of taking into account staff expenses, which are an important cost component in Europe, and has proven very robust in providing uniform results for different sizes of businesses in spite of its simplicity.

The following five ratios were found to impact predominantly the risk of bankruptcy:

R1 = EBITDA [= Earnings before interest, taxes, depreciation, and amortization] / Total debts
R2 = (Equity + Financial debts over 1 year) / Total assets
R3 = (Working assets – Inventory) / Total assets
R4 = Net interest expenses [= –Financial result] / Turnover
R5 = Staff expenses / Value added [= Turnover – Operational expenses paid to third parties]

The score is then calculated with the following coefficients:

$$Z_{CH} = 24*R1 + 22*R2 + 16*R3 - 87*R4 - 10*R5$$

The risk of distress within the next two years is expressed in scores as follows:

Figure 24. Statistical cut-off values for the Conan and Holder score

10%	16
20%	13
30%	11
40%	9
50%	7
60%	5
70%	3
80%	0
90%	−5
100%	−21

These commonly used cut-off values allow classifying each firm within a three-colour scheme:

Figure 25. Discriminant zones for Conan and Holder

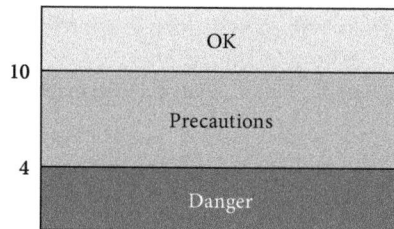

In other words, firms with a Conan and Holder score above 10 can be selected automatically, those with a score between 4 and 10 should be subject to in-depth financial analysis or an additional test, and those below 4 are not eligible if this criterion is used.

3. THE ALTMAN Z SCORES

The American researcher Edward Altman was the first to use discriminant analysis in business distress prediction in 1968. Since then, he and his fellow researchers have developed several scores called Z, Z', Z" and ZETA scores. These scores result from a very large sample of businesses in the United States and other developed and emerging markets and concern different types of companies, which can be relevant in particular for investors.

Public contracting authorities may be particularly interested in the Z" score which covers non-manufacturing businesses, and which is therefore independent from factors regarding inventory fluctuation. It is widely applicable to most types of procurement for public administrations.

The ratios influencing the distress probability are:

R1 = Working capital [= Current assets – Current liabilities] / Total assets
R2 = Retained earnings / Total assets
R3 = EBIT [= Operating result] / Total assets
R4 = Equity [book value or market value for exchange listed companies] / Total assets

and the score is:

$$Z'' = 6.56*R1 + 3.26*R2 + 6.72*R3 + 1.05*R4$$

The three-colour scheme for the probability of distress within two years as defined by Altman is as follows:

Figure 26. Discriminant zones for Altman Z"

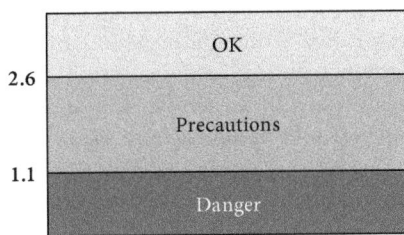

Again, firms with a Z" score above 2.6 can be selected automatically, those with a score between 1.1 and 2.6 should be subject to in-depth financial analysis or an additional test, and those below 1.1 are not eligible if this criterion is used.

4. THE PRACTICAL APPLICATION OF FINANCIAL HEALTH SCORING

4.1. DEFINING THE CRITERION

If we have chosen to address the risk of a contractor's bankruptcy through selection criteria, our relevant selection criterion will be "economic viability". For the sake of clarity and transparency, to inform firms what we will do and to allow them to see already for themselves whether they are eligible or not, the tender specifications should describe the applicable viability evaluation method. It should include the necessary margin of manoeuvre, meaning that firms may rely on the capacity of others to meet criteria they would not meet on their own, and meaning that, even if they do, we reserve the right to reject them nevertheless in case of serious and duly justified doubts as to their real capacity.

Scoring on its own may well be insufficient in case of vast projects of critical importance to the contracting authority, such as hospital concessions or major infrastructure projects. In that case a combination of scoring and an in-depth analysis, possibly contracted out to professional business analysts, can be envisaged. In everyday procurement, though, in the light of the cost-effectiveness of different forms of verification, we suggest the following example of an economic viability criterion:

Conan and Holder score of the last two closed financial years:

–   if the Y-1 and Y-2 scores are above 10, the firm is selected by default
–   if the Y-1 score is below 4, the firm is rejected by default
–   in the remaining cases:
    o   either an in-depth financial analysis is carried out, or
    o   the following tests are applied
        •   positive EBITDA in Y-1 and Y-2
        •   positive equity as of the end of Y-1

It makes very little if any sense to examine accounts older than two years, save for exceptional situations where we need to examine medium-term evolution of some figures for a specific purpose. Certainly during economic crises the financial situation of companies can change quickly and past accounting figures quickly become irrelevant. Even the last closed financial year reflects figures from the more or less recent past, as a closure of accounts, audit and vote by the shareholders are necessary. Year Y-2 is mostly interesting to check whether there are any major fluctuations or potential problems in the financing dynamics, not really to assess current financial health. This is also why more emphasis is put on the score of the last closed year in the proposed criterion.

The supplementary tests for companies whose scores do not allow for automatic selection or rejection – the "grey area" between black and white, or the "yellow zone" between red and green – are proposed in order to ensure a degree of continued user-friendly automation. Strictly speaking, an in-depth analysis would allow for a more accurate risk response. For example we may discover that short-term debt, which had been problematically high at the end of the last financial year, has in the meantime been transformed into long-term debt, so overall viability is in fact restored, or that structurally low capital can be explained by particular corporate financial arrangements. Yet if we lack the means, the time, or both to carry out such an analysis, the two supplementary tests for grey or yellow cases form at least an acceptable compromise between accuracy and ease of use. EBITDA, or gross earnings from the operating assets, should be positive in a sound corporation whatever the current conjuncture is, and net equity should also be positive, meaning that the company has not accumulated losses that exceed its capital.

But before publishing the method and its thresholds, grey or yellow or otherwise, we recommend testing them on known companies first. In fact, this should be done for any selection criterion: take the existing contractor company if we find it sufficiently capable, as well as a few other likely candidates, and simulate what scores they would obtain. If they all fail the test, it could mean that they are either all in critical situations, or that there is a peculiarity in the relevant sector or market segment. It is better to have these surprises at the drafting stage than to experience them after the opening of tenders or the observation that no-one actually tendered.

Figure 27. Screenshot of a simplified account sheet

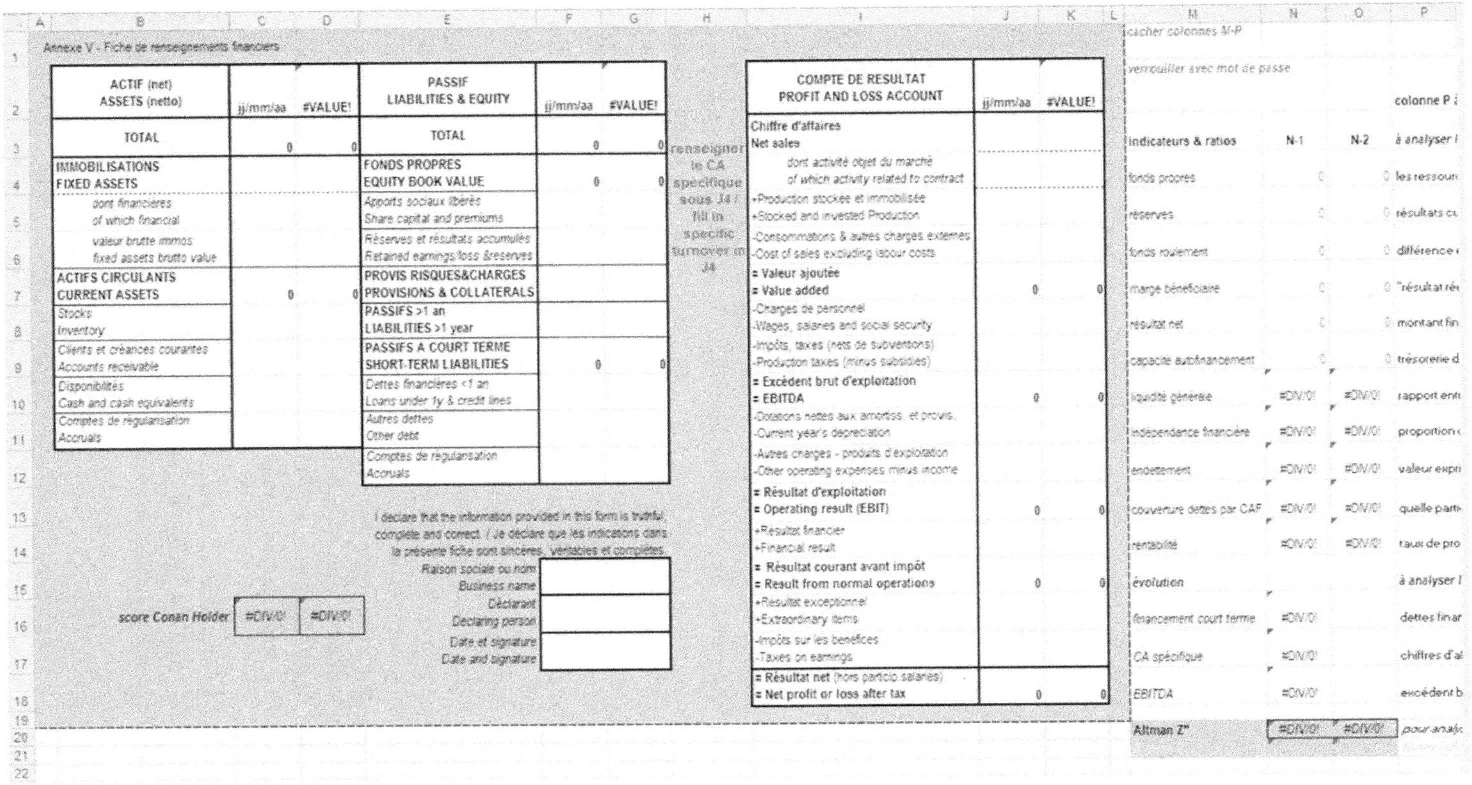

4.2.   REQUESTING PROOFS

Although the figures necessary to calculate the scores are available in the balance sheet and the profit-and-loss account, it can be time-consuming to retrieve and compile them, certainly if tenderers are established in another jurisdiction where a different language or different formats to present information apply. Moreover, if scores are not immediately visible to firms as they prepare their tender, some companies might misjudge their own capacity and submit a tender only to be rejected. For these reasons, we advocate the use of a simplified account sheet, with relevant subtotals from the balance sheet and the profit-and-loss account, that is provided in the form of a password-protected Excel spreadsheet that is part of the tendering documentation and that is filled in by the tenderers themselves. The sheet can calculate the score, to give tenderers an idea on how they stand in relation to financial capacity thresholds, and contain hidden columns with a dashboard of indicators that will help evaluators during further analysis if necessary. The only manual verification then consists in cross-checking a few figures from the balance sheet and the profit-and-loss account against the simplified account sheet, to make sure that the transcription is correct.

4.3.   ADVANTAGES, DRAWBACKS AND ALTERNATIVE APPROACHES

Manual financial analysis and scoring are not the only methods to assess the economic viability of companies. As noted, it is theoretically possible to rely on a single indicator, or a set of individual indicators. But, as also noted, we advise against it because the accuracy is too poor, resulting in too many "false positives" and "false negatives", meaning sick firms that get selected and healthy firms that are either rejected or that do not even tender.

A seemingly more sophisticated alternative is to define a set of ratios or other indicators, and to stipulate that firms must have satisfactory results on, for example, four out of five indicators. Yet while this looks similar to scoring, it is not, because scoring weights different indicators for their statistical importance, while four-out-of-five does not. For example, under scoring, a company that has high labour costs and a low EBITDA due to an immediate business problem can be, rightly, still considered healthy if it has a stable long-term financing of its operations. If we consider the ratios separately, however, two of them will already be in the red zone.

In spite of its advantages, we should also be clear about the drawbacks that scoring represents, or at least the further implications it entails.

–   Even in an "automated" setup, where the selection is carried out on the basis of thresholds and no "manual" analysis, the use of scoring requires some basic knowledge in accounting and financial analysis, especially in cases where tenderers with poor scores seek to rely on third-party capacity and other special situations. The procurement officer, or an evaluation committee member, should have these basics to avoid deadlocks during the selection procedure. As for other committee members and managers authorizing the expenditure, even if they cannot replicate an analysis themselves, they should at least understand the purpose of the analysis, the reason why the selection criterion had been included in the first place, and the meaning that any given scoring result represents.

- Scoring, with its very description and the requested financial information, might deter some companies that find it too complex, especially very small firms. We however recall that economic viability is a criterion most suited for longer contracts of a certain importance for business continuity, not for daily business and low-value one-off awards where it would be disproportionate. Even where we use it, though, we should not underestimate the financial expertise of businesses: scoring is a widely used method that the company's accountant will not only know from school, it is also part of his or her routine in dealing with clients, investors and banks. Nevertheless, it is absolutely necessary to be as clear and transparent as possible in the tender specifications about the method that will be applied, ideally in a way that allows firms to calculate or reasonably estimate their eligibility themselves.

If for any reason scoring cannot be used at all, but the contractor's financial health is nevertheless important to the contracting authority, we strongly recommend using only indicators that are most closely and objectively linked to actual financial health. Positive EBITDA, positive equity or positive net cash flow tend to make more sense than positive operating or net earnings, because the latter are influenced by pure accounting operations, notably amortization. Other potential alternatives are a threshold for profitability, that can however vary sharply according to sector and business size, or for short-term debt or a positive working capital, that can however be subject to economic conjuncture. The use of any of these indicators, including the risk from the lowered accuracy of the resulting viability estimates, should be weighed against the risk that it is meant to cover in the light of the nature of the contract.

APPENDIX II

MATHEMATICAL DISCUSSION OF FORMULAS TO DETERMINE PRICE-QUALITY RATIOS

In this book we propose to use a fair and simple formula to determine price-quality ratios in the award of public contracts, which is literally quality divided by price (Q/P). The formula is adjusted to the buyer's preferences in that all admissible tenders start out with a baseline quality score which corresponds to the price for basic acceptable quality in proportion to the maximum acceptable price for maximum useful quality. If we are willing to spend €60 on a basic product and up to €100 on the best, the basic quality price represents 60% of the maximum acceptable price, and we will spend 60% of theoretically available quality points just to attain basic quality. The weighting of award criteria, as it is published to let firms know the price elasticity of our demand, is 60:40 in favour of the price criterion. At the evaluation stage, if maximum useful quality is rewarded with 100 points in total, all technically compliant tenders are given 60 quality points and real quality competition will unfold over the remaining 40 points. Tenders' total quality scores will be spread between 60 and 100, and each tender will in the end have its total quality score divided by its own price, the highest ratio winning the award.

In this discussion we will first demonstrate why the weight-adjusted Q/P formula works. We will then demonstrate the disadvantages of another formula, one that is so far widely used by contracting authorities in Europe, which is a Q+P formula where prices are converted into points and where quality scores are added to, rather than divided by, the price score. Finally, we will consider – irrespective of the ratio formula – different methods to translate perceived quality into quality points.

1. THE ADJUSTMENT OF THE Q/P FORMULA TO THE WEIGHT OF THE PRICE CRITERION

If a raw, i.e. unadjusted, quality score is divided by the price offer, this simply means that the quality of tenders is assessed over 100% of the total quality scale. However the result for each tender is, in any case, a value-for-money ratio, namely the offered quality (on the vertical axis in the figure below) in relation to the price (represented on the horizontal axis). A linear curve crossing a tender represents all other hypothetical tenders with the same ratio: a tender that is twice as good and twice as expensive has the same ratio as one that is half as good and costs half as much. The winner is the tender that finds itself on the steepest curve, meaning that, irrespective of its absolute price and its absolute quality score, it offers most quality units per currency unit.

Figure 28. Q/P ratios with unadjusted quality scores

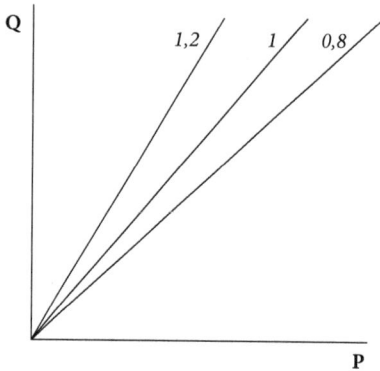

If, as is the case in the example above, the quality scores are not adjusted to the buyer's price elasticity, it means that the relative weight of the price criterion will always be equal to the relative weight of the quality criterion. Buyers may not always wish to establish such a 50:50 weighting, however, because they are not necessarily willing to pay twice as much for twice the quality. That is because, if most of what the buyer needs is already basic and mandatory quality according to the technical specifications, there is simply not that much quality margin left on which tenders can further distinguish themselves.

The figure below shows that even mere technical compliance, meaning minimum quality and no added quality, has a certain price. Based on market research, the buyer determines his or her estimate of what price corresponds to the basic solution that he or she is willing to accept. The buyer equally determines how much he or she would be willing to pay for maximum desirable quality – not necessarily based on known market prices, but rather as a monetary expression of the value, or utility, that this added quality would represent to him or her. The Q/P curve shown represents all hypothetical tenders with a price-quality ratio that the buyer will find acceptable at any given price. The curve rises more or less steeply, depending on the proportion of acceptable extra spending to the basic price. It crosses the quality axis not at 0, as was the case for unadjusted quality scores, but at a point that represents the price for minimum quality. Below that price the quality turns negative – meaning non-compliant with technical specifications – and the curve crosses the vertical axis at zero price and negative quality. This is the theoretical negative quality that costs nothing at all. The distance between the point at which the curve crosses the price axis and zero quality (s on the quality axis), in proportion to the distance between zero quality and maximum quality (v on the quality axis), is the same as the distance between zero price and basic price (s on the price axis) in proportion to the distance between basic price and maximum acceptable price (v on the price axis).

Figure 29. Q/P curve based on a price estimate for basic quality and the reservation price for maximum quality

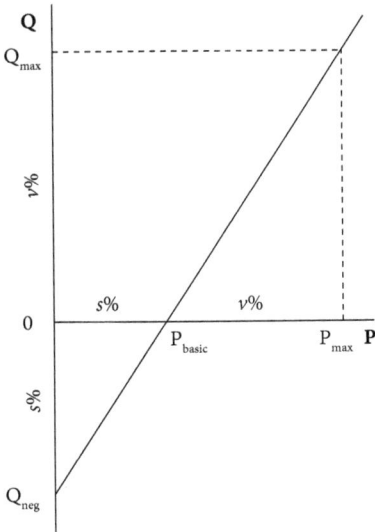

In order to calculate the price-quality ratios for each tender, the respective Q/P curves must nevertheless start from the origin, as they did with unadjusted quality scores. In other words, the point representing zero quality must be shifted downward to the negative quality at zero price (Q_{neg}). This is done by simply allocating to each tender s% of the overall quality score and by distributing the qualitative criteria points over the remaining v%. In the figure below, basic quality represents 40% of maximum quality, meaning that tenderers can fulfil 60% of total quality needs by meeting qualitative award criteria. Therefore, all technically compliant tenders receive 40% of available quality points from the start; basic quality will stay at 40%, while maximum quality can obtain up to 100% of quality points. When the total quality score is divided by the price, again the winner is the tender through which the steepest curve can be drawn.

Figure 30. Q/P curve adjusted for minimum quality requirements at 40:60 weighting

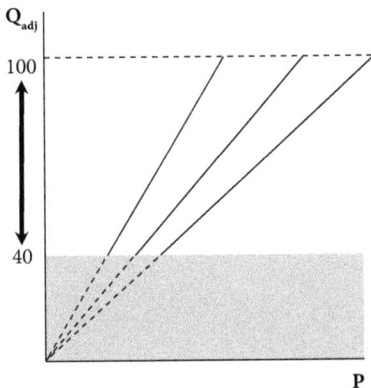

2.   THE DISADVANTAGES OF THE Q+P METHOD

Among the advantages of the Q/P formula with adjusted quality scores that we propose is the fact that it is, even if we consider just the purely mathematical level, fair and objective. It is fair notably because all tenderers have an equal chance of arriving at a good price-quality ratio, irrespective of the price range in which they compete; and it is objective because this ratio is calculated on the merits of each tender itself, irrespective of the content of the other tenders. We put this in stark contrast to another method, which we will call Q+P, where prices are converted into points as a function of the lowest bid received, where the price score is weighted in line with the published weighting of award criteria, and where that price score is added to the weighted quality score. We advise not to use this formula, or to stop using it, for a number of reasons. First, in its basic form, this formula systematically disadvantages mid-range prices. Second, below a certain quality score at a certain weighting, price differences and therefore the price criterion is completely cancelled out. Third, if tenders' final scores for both price and quality are added, awards are made without any regard to the winner's actual price-quality ratio, so awards can even go to tenderers at prices that are exaggerated in relation the quality they offer. Since the Q/P formula as we propose it does create a proper ratio, rather than a sum, and since it takes the price offer as it is, without converting it into points to begin with, it by definition avoids these flaws.

2.1.   THE PENALIZATION OF MID-RANGE TENDERS

A price score function – if the buyer feels the need to convert prices into points to begin with – should be fair to all admissible and technically compliant tenders, whatever the price range in which they compete. This is not the case under the following conversion formula to generate price scores:

$$\text{your price score} = (\text{lowest bid} / \text{your bid}) \times 100$$

This formula automatically awards the maximum price score to whichever tender is the cheapest – because its price gets divided by itself, resulting in a coefficient of 1 – and lower scores to everyone else as a function for their distance to the lowest bid. As soon as there are more than two tenderers, however, the formula results in a penalty for those who are between the highest and the lowest bid. In the example below, tender B is exactly half-way between A and C, but its score is not: under fair, i.e. linear conditions, it would receive 75 points, but in fact it receives only 67 (or 11% less than what would be fair). This penalty of eight points arbitrarily lowers B's chances of winning the contract, once quality scores are added to the price scores, just because its price happens to be mid-range.

Figure 31. Penalization of mid-range tenders in price scoring where the lowest bid is divided by price offers

Tender	Price	Applied formula	Price score
A	€50	(50 / 50) x 100	100
B	€75	(50 / 75) x 100	67 (!)
C	€100	(50 / 100) x 100	50

The penalty results from the fact that the formula is not a linear but a hyperbolic function. The penalty imposed on mid-range offers is particularly striking since, intuitively, if anything these should be privileged not disadvantaged against too basic or too expensive tenders. But in order to be just competitive with the most expensive tender, a mid-range tender must provide 11% more relative quality.

Figure 32. Price score curve if the lowest bid is divided by price offers

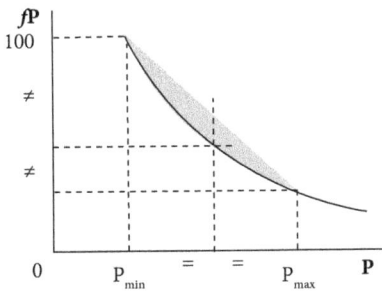

The area showing up grey is the visualization of the unfairness of the formula. We acknowledge that formulas adding price scores and quality scores do not necessarily use the described formula to convert prices into points. Conversion formulas exist that actually are linear. But then they still base the scores on tenders received, and they still result in a sum not a ratio, the more fundamental drawbacks of which we will discuss now.

2.2. THE NEUTRALIZATION OF THE PRICE CRITERION

As noted earlier in this book, the Q+P formula may lead to a neutralization of the price criterion in case the relative weight of the price criterion drops below 50%. This means a tender cannot compensate the quality spread between tenders by its price, even though it is perfectly compliant with the tender specifications. The reason is, in short, that the competition is over if the number of theoretically available price points is lower than the quality difference between two tenders: a tender whose quality score is 31 points lower than that of a competitor cannot make up the difference via a low price if there are only 30 price points available in total. Shown below is an equivalence table for Q/P criteria weights, using the method described earlier, and the corresponding criteria weights under Q+P. On the right are listed the quality weights that would need to be fixed under the Q+P formula in order to generate evaluation results that correspond to the actual price elasticity of the buyer's demand. Such correspondence of results and demand is achieved when the basic product at a basic price and the best product at the maximum price both receive the same final score in the end, in the way Q/P generates equal price-quality ratios for them because they both offer equivalent quality solutions in different price ranges.

Figure 33. Equivalence for quality weights under Q/P and Q+P formulas

Q/P		Q+P
Basic solution value = baseline score	Quality criteria weight	Quality criteria weight
1.00	0.00	0.00
0.95	0.05	0.05
0.90	0.10	0.09
0.85	0.15	0.13
0.80	0.20	0.17
0.75	0.25	0.20
0.70	0.30	0.23
0.65	0.35	0.26
0.60	0.40	0.29
0.55	0.45	0.31
0.50	0.50	0.33
0.45	0.55	0.35
0.40	0.60	0.38
0.35	0.65	0.39
0.30	0.70	0.41
0.25	0.75	0.43
0.20	0.80	0.44
0.15	0.85	0.46
0.10	0.90	0.47
0.05	0.95	0.49
0.00	1.00	0.50

We can see that the weighting under Q+P is different, as it does not take into account overall quality, reserving instead half the points for the best quality and the other half for the best price. A firm offering perfect quality and an exorbitant price should then get the maximum 50 points for quality and (close to) 0 points for price, whereas simple compliance with tender specifications and an extremely low price should be awarded 0 points for (added) quality and 50 points for the price, in order to remain on the same curve of price-quality ratio equivalence. The result of this logic is that the quality weight tends to 0.5, instead of 1.0, where the tender specifications have no intrinsic value, where everything depends on qualitative award criteria and where nothing depends on the price.

So what happens if the price weight drops below 50% and the weighting is, say, 30:70 in favour of the quality criteria? It means that any tender with over 30 quality points less than the best quality tender is out of the competition, whatever the prices are. It simply becomes impossible to overcome the quality score gap via a competitive price, because there are not enough price points available to do so. If we trace this weighting on a graph similar to the ones used earlier, it shows the following:

Figure 34. Q/P curve for a case of preponderant quality weight under a Q+P formula

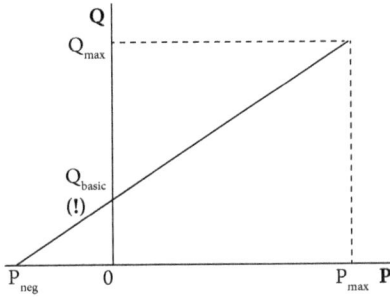

When the price weight is below 50%, the Q/P score does not cross the quality axis below 0 but above. In other words, apparently a zero euro tender already has a positive quality value to us. Also, any tender that is technically compliant but receives a score below Q_{basic}, meaning a score below the crossing point of the Q/P curve on the quality axis, is out of the game because it is treated as if it had a negative price.

How do contracting authorities using a preponderant quality weight manage to make plausible awards under such circumstances? Presumably there are two explanations. First, the Q_{basic} score, corresponding to the quality weight minus the price weight, may effectively be used as an implicit minimum quality threshold. Tenderers that fail to attain the minimum score are in reality rejected for having insufficient quality, not for being too expensive in relation to the quality. However in this case the quality threshold should be disclosed in the tender documents in full transparency, and it should result from objectively defined minimum quality levels, not from an unintended side-effect of a formula. Second, evaluators may be officially using the whole available quality range but in reality give points in such a way that all tenders end up in a narrow range of scores. If there is a $P_{30}:Q_{70}$ weighting on paper but in practice all tenders receive between 40 and 60 points for quality, then the effective weighting in a Q+P formula is 20:30, or $P_{60}:Q_{40}$. In other words, in both cases the inherent unfairness of the formula for sellers is mitigated by the inadequate evaluation techniques of the buyers, which is not a very convincing way of awarding contracts. Again, we suggest using the Q/P formula instead, so that low-end tenderers can legitimately compensate their quality score with a better price, generating a good ratio, and so that the degree to which this is possible depends on the buyer's preferences and not on whether there are enough price points left.

2.3. THE DEPENDENCE OF EFFECTIVE CRITERIA WEIGHTS ON THE PRICING LEVEL

Whereas a Q/P formula allows allocating an objective value-for-money ratio to any tender received, this is not the case under the Q+P method. Let us assume two scenarios: we receive tenders A and B that have a given quality (60 and 80 out of 100, respectively), but in one scenario with lower absolute prices (€100 and €120) and in another with higher absolute prices but in the same proportion to each other (€150 and €180).

Figure 35. Evaluation results in different pricing configurations

Tender	Quality	Price 1	Q/P	$Q_{50}+P_{50}$	Price 2	Q/P	$Q_{50}+P_{50}$
A	60%	€100	0.6	30+50 = 80	€150	0.4	30+50 = 80
B	80%	€120	0.67	40+42 = 82	€180	0.44	40+42 = 82

We see that the Q/P formula, since it calculates actual ratios, generates a different score depending on the absolute price level. This is logical, since higher absolute prices at constant quality must evidently result in a poorer price-quality ratio. Yet the Q+P formula, which for the price score makes itself dependent on the relative price differences between offers received, will always show the same score, no matter how high prices are in absolute terms.

This effect has certain consequences for the award decision. First, we may end up paying more in absolute terms for quality aspects because the maximum price score under Q+P formulas does not actually correspond to a monetary counterpart but simply to the lowest price among the received tenders. Second, under such circumstances we cannot set in advance our internal acceptability threshold for tenders. Intuitively, and quite correctly, a tender that offers 80% of maximum desirable quality and costs €120 is not exactly the same as a tender that offers the same quality but costs €180. The Q/P formula, which shows value for money, will immediately display the difference; Q+P, by contrast, which only shows relative price differences between the tenders and no proportion to the quality, only a sum, will display the same score in both cases. Thus we cannot compare the score to a value-for-money benchmark in case we receive only one tender, and we cannot express via our score the unreasonableness of prices, in relation to offered quality, in case of oligopolistic markets.

3. QUALITY SCORE AS A FUNCTION OF ACTUAL QUALITY

To make a Q/P calculation, in fact to use any formula that expresses quality in a numerical score, we must first translate quality into points. This means that there is a function to express how the actual quality is quantified and distributed on a scale between 0 and a maximum number of points. Whenever we speak of quality for the purpose of generating ratios, we are therefore in fact speaking of a quality score that is a function of real quality.

$$Q = f Q_{actual}$$

This function can be defined in a relatively implicit way, by determining methods or guidelines for evaluators to grade quality, or by an explicit formula that awards a quality score to measurable quality aspects such as duration, weight, time of assembly, etc. Yet however the function is defined, we need to realize that the explicit formula does not necessarily have to be linear, and that human evaluators are not likely to grade quality in a perfectly linear way either. The reason for that is a phenomenon that economists call diminishing marginal utility, meaning that from a certain point onwards each further increase in quality is worth less and less to us.

In a "barebones" product, for example, an increment in quality brings an important increase of usefulness for us. However, as the quality rises further, we obtain less and less advantage from each subsequent quality increment: the curve representing the quality function rises steeply and then flattens out. This describes many phenomena in everyday consumer life. For example, having eaten a certain amount of ice cream, we will enjoy each additional portion less and less. In other words, the utility difference between having *no* ice cream and having *some* ice cream tends to be considerable; the difference between one portion and two portions is already less pronounced; the difference between the fourth and the fifth portion is negligible. Similarly, a mobile phone with an in-built camera can represent a great quality advantage over a phone that has no camera at all, but additional excitement will not continue to rise linearly with each additional megapixel. A product warranty of five years may be better than one of two years, but eight years instead of five will probably not feel twice as good, even though the increment in the number of years was the same in both cases.

Figure 36. Concave and capped quality function in tender evaluation

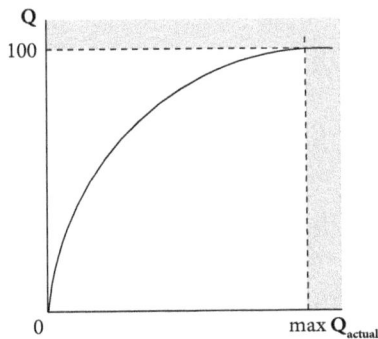

Again, human evaluators using comprehensible but non-rigid evaluation techniques will naturally assign differences in quality scores that are higher between 10 and 20 than they are between 90 and 100 on the actual quality axis. If the scoring is carried out in a rigid, linear fashion because there is a fixed assessment grid that transposes quantitative values into points, however, scores will not accurately reflect the buyer's preferences. Giving the same number of points for going from 90 to 100 actual quality as for going from 10 to 20 means overvaluing, and overpaying for, quality increases towards maximum utility, while undervaluing quality increments in the basic range. While for simple low-stakes awards the inaccuracy of a linear function at the two extremes of the curve might be tolerable, it may become too distortive from the buyer's point of view when stakes are high. In such cases we recommend adjusting the quality scoring curve to come closer to the buyer's real utility curve, in that assessment grids, if they must develop a certain level of detail, provide for different point ranges at different segments of actual quality.

In any case the quality curve must be capped at some point, because buyers are unlikely to wish to pay indefinitely for ever higher quality beyond its maximum usefulness. Quality scores should "max out" at maximum utility, for example when the number of years of product warranty starts exceeding the expected lifetime of the product itself: additional warranty beyond that time should be worth nothing at all to the buyer. A linear curve intrapolating tenders between basic quality and maximum utility will simply stop at that point; a curve that resembles realistically human preferences more closely will flatten out before stopping altogether the score growth in relation to quality growth.

REFERENCES

E.I. Altman, 'Revisiting Credit Scoring Models in a Basel II Environment', in: M.K. Ong, ed., *Credit Ratings: Methodologies, Rationale and Default Risk*, London: Risk Books 2002.

E.I. Altman, Predicting Financial Distress Of Companies: Revisiting The Z-Score And Zeta® Models, NYU Working Paper, July 2000.

A.R. Apostol, 'Public procurement of innovation – A structural approach', *Public Procurement Law Review* (2012).

S. Arrowsmith, 'EC Regime on Public Procurement', in K. Thai, ed., *International Handbook of Public Procurement*, Boca Raton, CRC Press 2009.

Chr. Bovis, *EU Public Procurement Law*, 2nd ed., Cheltenham: Edward Elgar 2012.

J. Conan & M. Holder, *Variables explicatives de performance et contrôle de gestion dans les P.M.I.*, Paris: CERG, Université Paris Dauphine 1979.

N. Dimitri, 'Best Value for Money in Procurement', *Journal of Public Procurement* (2013), pp. 149–175.

European Commission, *Risk Management in the Commission, Implementation Guide*, internal document of the European Commission, version November 2013, Annex 1.

ISO, *International Standard ISO 9000: Quality Management Systems – Fundamentals and Vocabulary*, Geneva: ISO Copyright Office 2005.

J.L. Fuentes-Bargues & C. González-Gaya, 'Analysis of the scoring formula of economic criteria in public works procurement', *International Journal of Economic Behavior and Organization* (2013), pp. 1–12.

P. Jouannet, *Techniques de négociation dans l'achat public, niveau 2* (training material), Paris: ACP 2014.

Ph. Kiiver & J. Kodym, 'Price-Quality Ratios in Value-for-Money Awards', *Journal of Public Procurement* (2015), forthcoming.

K. Krüger, 'Ban-on-Negotiations in Tender Procedures: Undermining the Best Value for Money', in K. Thai, ed., *International Handbook of Public Procurement*, Boca Raton, CRC Press 2009.

W. Lawther, 'Contract Negotiations', in K. Thai, ed., *International Handbook of Public Procurement*, Boca Raton, CRC Press 2009.

K. Lundvall, J. Tops & H. Ballebye Olesen, *What can public procurers learn from private?*, Copenhagen Economics 2008, p. 26.

L. Mandru et al., 'The diagnosis of bankruptcy risk using score function', in: *Proceedings of the 9th WSEAS international conference on artificial intelligence, knowledge engineering and data bases (AIKED'10)*, Stevens Point: WSEAS 2010, pp. 83–87.

R.D. Moen & C.L. Norman, 'Circling Back: Clearing up myths about the Deming cycle and seeing how it keeps evolving', *Quality Progress*, November 2010, p. 22–28.

OECD, *Integrity in Public Procurement*, Paris: OECD 2007.

S. Onderstal & F. Felsö, 'Procurement Design: Lessons from Economic Theory and Illustrations from the Dutch Procurement of Welfare-to-Work Projects', in K. Thai, ed., *International Handbook of Public Procurement*, Boca Raton: CRC Press 2009.

PWC EU Services / Utrecht University, *Public procurement: Costs we pay for corruption*, 2013.

P. Trepte, *Public Procurement in the EU – A Practitioner's Guide*, 2nd ed., Oxford: OUP 2007.

F. Waara & J. Bröchner, 'Price and Nonprice Criteria for Contractor Selection', *Journal of Construction Engineering and Management* (2006), pp. 797–804.

INDEX*

---

*   Numbers refer to the first page of the relevant section.

Lightning Source UK Ltd.
Milton Keynes UK
UKHW031833171220
375438UK00009B/634

9 781780 682662